A Photographic Guide to

TREES

OF BRITAIN AND EUROPE

Paul Sterry and Bob Press

NEW HOLLAND

First published in the UK in 1995 by
New Holland (Publishers) Ltd
Chapel House, 24 Nutford Place, London W1H 6DQ

ISBN 1 85368 259 4

Editor: Charlotte Fox
Designed and typeset by D & N Publishing, Ramsbury, Wiltshire

Reproduction by Modern Age Repro Co Ltd, Hong Kong
Printed and bound in Singapore by Tien Wah Press (Pte) Ltd

Front cover photograph: English Elm (Paul Sterry)
Back cover photograph: Cabbage Palm (Paul Sterry)
Title page photograph: Holly berries (Paul Sterry)

Photographic acknowledgements
All the photographs in this book were supplied by Nature Photo-
graphers Ltd. Most were taken by Andrew Cleave, the exceptions
being the following: SC Bisserot 32u, 34u, 55u, 97l; Frank V
Blackburn 18u, 79u; Brinsley Burbidge 15u, 15l, 16u, 18m, 28u,
30u, 36ll, 59l, 75l, 97u, 106l, 119u; Robin Bush 135ur; NA Cal-
low 26u; Geoff du Feu 75u; Christopher Grey-Wilson 61u, 121u;
Jean Hall 100ul; David Hawes 53ul; EA Janes 44l, 91ll, 96u; Tony
Schilling 19l; Paul Sterry 14l, 24u, 25ul, 25ur, 25l, 31l, 34l, 38u,
41u, 41m, 43u, 46ll, 46lr, 52ul, 52ur, 54lr, 55l, 58l, 60l, 61ll, 62u,
62m, 63u, 63l, 67ul, 67m, 67l, 74l, 76u, 81l, 82u, 82m, 85u, 87u,
87m, 91ll, 93ll, 93lr, 107u, 108ll, 108lr, 112l, 116l, 118l, 120u,
120l, 122ur, 127ll, 127lr, 128u, 131u, 132l, 134ul, 134ur, 134lr,
137l; Roger Tidman 104u, 104l; Andrew Weston 135ul.
u = upper, l = lower, m = middle, ul = upper left, ur = upper right
ll = lower left, lr = lower right.

Contents

Introduction

Wherever they grow, trees dominate the landscape and exert an attraction to people with wide-ranging interests from natural history to gardening. Defining exactly what constitutes a tree, however, can be rather difficult since examples come from almost all plant families; the group characteristically being woody and generally large in size. Trees may grow in solitary and magnificent splendour or en masse, blanketing the terrain. In whatever situation they are found, however, they are a unique and fascinating group.

Trees are usually defined as having a single large and well-developed trunk which branches well above ground. Shrubs on the other hand have a smaller and more diffuse habit with several stems branching at or near ground level. These differences are, however, somewhat arbitrary and the distinctions are often further blurred in cultivated or managed settings by man's interference with the tree's natural habit. This book, therefore, covers almost all the trees, or species popularly thought of as trees, from Europe as well as larger shrubs. Native, naturalised and popularly cultivated species are included.

The geographical range covered by this book extends from the Arctic tundra south to the Mediterranean Sea and from the Atlantic Ocean eastwards to a line running from the Ural Mountains to the Caspian Sea. Within this region, however, it can be rather problematical to define the precise ranges occupied by many tree species. Under natural conditions, trees are influenced by physical boundaries such as mountain ranges or seas, rather than lines on maps. Many trees, however, have had their natural distributions radically altered by man as a result of planting for timber or ornament.

This book is intended to help the tree enthusiast by both providing an effective guide to most species encountered in Europe, along with information on structure, habit, natural history and distribution of trees. Their attraction is enhanced by an understanding of how, why and where trees grow and an ability to distinguish between them and put a name to each specimen encountered.

How to use this book

The main part of this book is devoted to species descriptions and runs from page 14 to page 139. Each species is illustrated with a colour photograph beside which is informative text that will help identify the tree and provide useful and interesting background information. The species are arranged according to families and in an order that follows the convention of most other guides and definitive works on tree classification.

The photographs

With all species entries included in this book, at least one colour photograph is included to illustrate the tree in question. The photographs have been selected to show the most useful aspects of the tree for identification purposes. In some cases, therefore, the illustration may show a whole tree while with others, leaves, flowers, fruit or bark may be included in the image.

Wherever possible, at least one whole tree image has been included for each tree family since this grouping often shares an overall characteristic shape. However, there is a danger in placing too greater emphasis on the usefulness of tree shape in specific identification. This is partly because of this same shared family character but, perhaps more significantly, because there is great variability in shape within species. This can be the result of age differences although trees also vary greatly according to where they grow. Man also frequently alters the natural shape by pruning and lopping branches. While overall shape may be variable, factors such as leaf size and shape are much more constant.

The descriptions

The descriptions provide detailed information about each tree. The first entry is the popular, or common name which is printed in bold; some trees have no common name in English. The scientific name comes next and is printed in italics. Although the common name will obviously vary from country to country and between languages, the scientific name remains constant and therefore provides and effective means of communication between tree enthusiasts from anywhere in the world.

The next entry refers to the height that the tree normally attains in maturity; the emphasis here is on the word normally. Some individuals may be smaller or larger than the figures shown but most will fall into this category. The reader should also bear in mind that smaller trees may simply be growing specimens that have not yet reached maturity. If not otherwise stated then a tree is deciduous, that is it sheds its leaves in the autumn.

Within the species descriptions, the order of the text in most cases follows a standard sequence describing the various parts of the plant where appropriate: trunk, crown, bark, branches and twigs, leaves and stipules, inflorescence and flowers, and fruits. A flowering period is given but, like the tree height, it represents a range only. It can vary widely for any given species depending on where in the continent an individual tree is growing and altitude, as well as local fluctuations in the timing of the seasons. The greatest variation occurs with trees which have a broad north–south geographical range, or which are found from the mild Atlantic coasts to the more continental climate of eastern and central Europe.

Species descriptions end with an indication of the distribution of the tree in Europe and, for introduced species, their country of origin; an indication of their relative frequency and any relevant ecological factors or major uses is also given where appropriate.

Corner tabs

These provide an at-a-glance reference relating to the species family groups. See key below.

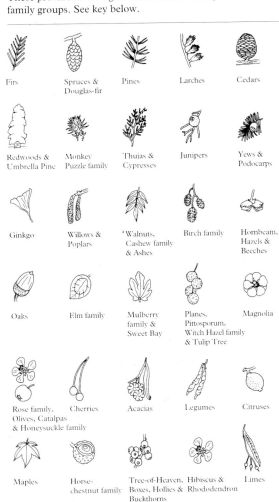

Firs

Spruces & Douglas-fir

Pines

Larches

Cedars

Redwoods & Umbrella Pine

Monkey Puzzle family

Thujas & Cypresses

Junipers

Yews & Podocarps

Ginkgo

Willows & Poplars

Walnuts, Cashew family & Ashes

Birch family

Hornbeam, Hazels & Beeches

Oaks

Elm family

Mulberry family & Sweet Bay

Planes, Pittosporum, Witch Hazel family & Tulip Tree

Magnolia

Rose family, Olives, Catalpas & Honeysuckle family

Cherries

Acacias

Legumes

Citruses

Maples

Horse-chestnut family

Tree-of-Heaven, Boxes, Hollies & Buckthorns

Hibiscus & Rhododendron

Limes

Tupelo family & Gums

Pomegranate, Dogwood & Heather families

Palms

Glossary

Alternate With one leaf alternately at each stem joint.

Anther Fertile part of a stamen, containing pollen.

Aril Fleshy layer covering the seed of some trees.

Bract Leaf-like organ beneath a flower or inflorescence, sometimes modified or very reduced in size.

Burrs Numerous short, twiggy outgrowths from the trunk.

Calyx All the sepals of a flower.

Capsule Dry fruit splitting when ripe to release seeds.

Catkin Slender inflorescence of small, usually wind-pollinated flowers.

Corolla All the petals of a flower.

Crown All the branches of a tree.

Cultivar Type of plant developed by gardeners, not originiating in the wild.

Cupule Cup-shaped structure enclosing a fruit or fruits.

Deflexed Bent backwards.

Glabrous Smooth and hairless.

Inflorescence A group of flowers and their particular arrangement e.g. a spike or cluster.

Involucre Leaf-like structure enclosing a flower.

Lenticel Pore in a trunk, twig or sometimes fruit, allowing the passage of gases to a from the tissues.

Opposite With a pair of leaves at each joint on the stem.

Ovary Female organ of the flower containing ovules.

Palmate With lobes or leaflets spreading from a single point.

Papillae Slender outgrowths resembling hairs.

Perianth The sepals and petals of a flower.

Petiole Leaf stalk.

Pinna One of the primary divisions of a pinnate leaf.

Pinnate With two parallel rows of lobes or leaflets.

Rachis Central axis of a pinnate leaf to which leaflets are attached.

Sepals Outermost whorl of floral parts, often green.

Stamen Male organ of a flower.

Stigma Sticky area on the ovary, receptive to pollen.

Stipule Leaf-like organ at the base of a petiole.

Sucker New shoot growing from roots of the parent tree.

Style Elongated part of the ovary bearing the stigma.

Trifoliate With three leaflets.

Tree names and classification

Scientists studying classification divide all plants, including trees, into groups based on characters common to all members, and the groups are arranged in a hierarchy. The most frequently used ranks are described below.

The basic unit of classification is the species. This is generally regarded as a group of individuals which possess common characteristics clearly distinguishing them from other groups. They must also be capable of breeding together to produce viable offspring; unlike animals, closely related species of plants can often interbreed and produce viable offspring.

Within the species there may be considerable minor variation between individuals; if sufficiently marked and consistent these differences are used to define subspecies or varieties. Cultivars are horticulturally derived trees with characters not found in wild populations.

Closely related species are grouped into a genus and genera into a family, a useful division widely used by botanists when referring to plants. Some families contain only tree species, others contain annual and perennial herbs as well as shrubs and trees.

All families belong to one of two divisions, gymnosperms and angiosperms. Gymnosperms are plants with naked seeds and include all the cone-bearing trees such as Pines and Cypresses. Angiosperms have seeds protected ty an ovary and include all plants commonly referred to as flowering plants; the trees in this group are generally referred to as broadleaved.

Most trees in this book have one or even several common names. These, however, vary from country to country and between languages which can result in some confusion. In common with all living organisms known to science, all trees also have scientific names which are the same the world over.

Tree structure and identification

Taken as a whole, trees are very variable plants with almost all features or characters differing between species to a greater or lesser extent. When identifying trees, it is important to recognise the structures you are examining and to be sure you are comparing like with like. With this in mind, at least a basic understanding of the structure of trees and their component parts is essential. This next section will help in this respect.

Trunk and bark
Trees are woody plants with a well-developed trunk or bole. Together with the main branches, this is covered in a layer of bark which protects the tree from the outside environment. Trees grow in girth as well as height, adding additional layers

of woody tissue each year; these result in the annual rings seen when a trunk is cut. To accomodate this expansion in girth, the bark may stretch and rupture. The resulting patterns or flakings can be useful in identification.

Leaves

Leaves are the sites for food production and gas-exchange and are vitally important to the tree. The shape and arrangement of the leaves are often characteristic and are usually useful in identification. Most trees have leaves alternating on the twig but some have opposite pairs or whorls of leaves.

Many trees have simple leaves with a single blade although this may be pinnately or palmately lobed without being divided into leaflets. The blade shape can vary enormously between species, from narrow and laneolate to almost circular. Leaf shape is obviously important in identification but other useful

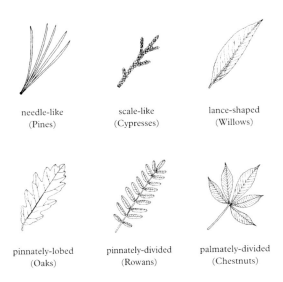

needle-like
(Pines)

scale-like
(Cypresses)

lance-shaped
(Willows)

pinnately-lobed
(Oaks)

pinnately-divided
(Rowans)

palmately-divided
(Chestnuts)

clues include the nature of the margin ie. whether it is unbroken on toothed, the colour, texture and hairiness. Conifers have leathery leaves which are either narrow and needle-like or scale-like, overlapping and pressed against the shoot.

Some trees have compound leaves divided into several leaflets. In pinnate leaves the leaflets lie in two parallel rows, usually with an odd leaflet at the tip. Twice-pinnate leaves have each initial division itself pinnately divided. In palmate leaves, the leaflets radiate from the/ petiole or leaf-stalk like fingers on a hand.

A particularly obvious division is between deciduous and evergreen trees. Deciduous trees shed all their leaves annually at the onset of the harshest season. In Europe this is usually winter, the trees avoiding cold weather and eliminating waste products accumulated in the leaves. For some trees from warm areas it may be the dry season – a water conservation measure. Evergreens also shed their leaves, but more gradually, constantly replacing lost leaves.

Crown

As it grows, the tree branches form a crown and the branching pattern can be a distinctive identification aid. The shape of the crown may change as the tree grows, however, and so the age of tree should be borne in mind. Young Cedars-of-Lebanon, for example, are spire-shaped but old trees are flat-topped and spreading. Conifers tend to grow quickly, often producing regular whorls of branches around the trunk, creating a conical shape. Broad-leaved trees are frequently slower growing, branching irregularly and producing a variety of crown shapes. Palms are unusual in having no branches: the crown is composed solely of leaves crowded at the top of the trunk. Twigs also vary with age, first-year twigs often being a different colour to older growth.

Flowers

Flowers are the reproductive organs of trees. They are made up of successive whorls of sepals, petals, stamens and ovaries, although any of these parts may be modified or absent. Sepals (collectively the calyx) and petals (the corolla) provide most clues to identify, especially in their number, size and colour. Parts of these whorls may be fused and where petals and sepals are indistinguishable from each other, they are referred to as perianth segments.

Flowers may be male, female or hermaphrodite and separate sex flowers are sometimes borne in separate clusters or even separate trees. Other factors to consider when using flowers for identification include whether they are solitary or grouped in some way.

Cone-bearing trees or conifers have male and female cones instead of flowers and fruits. Male cones are small and yellow when shedding pollent. The larger female cones comprise scales bearing egg-cells; when ripe they are woody.

Fruits

Fruits of non-coniferous trees fall into two broad categories, fleshy and juicy, or dry. Fleshy and juicy fruits include all berries and berry-like fruits as well as firm fruits such as apples. Dry fruits include pods, capsules and nuts. A few have woody, cone-like fruits. Fruits or seeds may be winged or have a parachute of hairs to aid dispersal by the wind.

Trees and man

Man has profound influence on the distribution and species occurrence of trees in Europe. This influence is not only historical but continues to this day in the form of felling, large-scale replanting, often with non-native species, and the growing of trees for ornament.

Of all Europe's forest types, the northern coniferous forest were, in the past, least disrupted by man. This was partly due to where they grow and also because they tended to occur on poor soils with little agricultural potential. Increasingly nowadays, however, their value as a source of timber is being exploited.

Man's influence on broad-leaved woodlands has been more noticeable. For several thousands of years woodlands have been cleared to create farming land and dwelling sites, and timber has been exploited for fuel and construction. By the time of the Domesday Book (1086), the present distribution of Britain's forests was largely in place. Those forests that remained were often managed in a sustainable fashion for timber and coppice produccts. Although Britain is one of the least wooded parts of Europe, similar processes of clearance were performed throughout much of Europe, albeit at much slower paces in most regions.

Mediterranean evergreen forests suffered most of all from man's acitivities. Some were managed, but the majority were ravaged by a combination of clearance, fire and grazing pressure of goats. Degraded forests form one of two vegetation types nowadays. Maquis, which occurs mainly on limestone has stunted trees but is dominated by aromatic shrubs. Garigue is poorer still with small shrubs but no trees at all.

Man has also helped to spread trees beyond their normal ranges and introduce foreign ones from beyond the borders of Europe. Ancient examples include the Carob which was introduced so long ago that its native distribution is almost completely obscured. The origins of Sweet Chestnut, Date Palm, Medlar and Orange are also poorly defined. More recently, alien conifer species and even Eucalyptus trees have been introduced for cheap timber and the list of cultivated species is almost endless.

Where to see trees in Europe

There are numerous gardens and arboreta throughout Europe where collections of trees can be seen, invariably offering a wider selection of species than would be found in natural woodland in the region. The following are just a very small selection of these, all open to the public.

Austria
1. Alpengarten Franz Mayr–Melnhof, Frohnleiten

Belgium
2. Arboretum, Kalmthout
3. Arboretum Geographicque, Overjise

Denmark
4. The Forest Botanical Garden, Århus

Where to see trees in Europe. The numbers relate to the sites mentioned in the text.

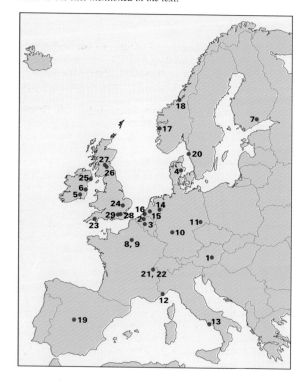

Eire
5. The John F. Kennedy Park, New Ross, County Wexford
6. National Botanical Gardens, Dublin

Finland
7. Arboretum Mustila, Elimäki

France
8. Arboretum et Alpinetum Vilmorin, Verrières-le-Buisson, just outside Paris
9. Museum National d'Histoire Naturelle, Jardin des Plantes, Paris

Germany
10. Botanische Garten der Johannes Gutenberg-Universitat Mainz, Mainz
11. Forstbotanischer Garten der Technischen Universitat Dresden Sektion

Italy
12. Giardino Botanico Hanbury, Latte
13. Orto Botanico di Napoli, Naples

Netherlands
14. Arboretum 'Poort-Bulten', DeLutte bij Oldenzaal
15. University Botanic Gardens, Utrecht
16. Stichting Arboretum Trombenburg, Rotterdam

Norway
17. The Norwegian Arboretum, Store Milde, near Bergen
18. Ringve Botaniske Hage, Trondheim

Spain
19. Real Jardin Botanico, Madrid

Sweden
20. Goteborgs Botaniska Tradgard, Gothenburg

Switzerland
21. Conservatoire et Jardin botaniques, Geneva
22. Jardin Alpin d'Aclimatation Floraire, Geneva

United Kingdom
23. Bicton Gardens, East Budleigh, Devon
24. Cambridge University Botanic Gardens, Cambridge
25. Dawyck Arboretum, Stobo, Peebles, Scotland
26. Castlewellan, Newcastle, Co. Down, N. Ireland
27. Royal Botanic Garden, Edinburgh, Scotland
28. Royal Botanic Gardens, Kew, Surrey
29. Wisley Gardens, Woking, Surrey

Noble Fir *Abies procera* 40 to 50m, sometimes more

This tall and attractive fir is stout and narrowly conical with horizontally spreading branches and pale grey bark. Cones are 12 to 20cm long. The young twigs are reddish, hairy and the buds are resinous only at their tips. Bluish-green needles are 10 to 35mm long. They are pressed against the shoot before curving upwards, leaving a parting below the shoot. A western North American species tolerant of exposed sites and poor soils. It is planted in northern and western Europe for timber and ornament.

Common Silver Fir *Abies alba* Up to 50m

A spiky, ragged crown distinguishes this evergreen tree. Pyrimidal to narrowly conical in shape with smooth, greyish bark cracking with age. Young twigs are densely hairy. Flexible needles are 15 to 30 × 1.5 to 2mm, and are flattened and slightly notched; they are blue-green with two silvery bands below. The cones are 10 to 20cm long, erect, and cylindrical. They are green ripening to brown and have a deflexed bract below each scale. Forms extensive natural forests from northern Spain to eastern Poland and the Balkans and is widely planted for timber in northern and western Europe.

Grecian Fir *Abies cephalonica* Up to 30m

An attractive tree with a stout and pyramidal crown and stiff and prickly leaves. The young twigs are glabrous and the buds are very resinous. The thick, flattened needles are 15 to 35mm long and are rigid and spine-tipped. They spread out evenly on either side of the shoot to leave a distinct parting above but a less distinct parting below. The cones are 12 to 16cm long and erect, with a deflexed bract beneath each scale. Native to the high mountains in Greece. It is also planted for timber in Italy and is grown ornamentally elsewhere in Europe.

Nikko Fir *Abies homolepis* Up to 27m

This tree has a roughly triangular but rather irregular crown. The young twigs are glabrous while the buds are very resinous. The needles are 25mm, rather stiff and flattened, rounded or notched at the tips and have two white bands beneath. They spread straight out to leave a distinct parting above the shoot. Cones are 8cm long and erect. They ripen from purple to brown, are often streaked with white resin and have bracts concealed by the cone scales. Native to Japan and is often planted in or near towns because of its pollution-resistant qualities.

15

Balsam Fir *Abies balsamea* Up to 25m

This hardy fir has a narrowing, spire-shaped crown. Young twigs are glabrous with resinous red buds. Needles are short, stiff and flattened. They are about 25mm long, blunt or notched at the tip and shiny green above but with two white bands beneath. Leaves spread forward along the shoots and are raised at an angle. The cones are 7cm long and egg-shaped, the bracts being almost concealed by the cone scales. A native of north to eastern North America and a scarce ornamental tree in Europe. The timber is economically important and the bark resin yields Canada Balsam.

Colorado White Fir *Abies concolor* Up to 30m

This is an extremely attractive fir, especially when seen in ornamental collections. The needles are medium length, fleshy and give off a citrus smell when rubbed; they curve upwards and away from the shoot and are rather bluish in colour but sometimes green on the upper surface. Cones are 8 to 10cm long, rather cylindrical in shape and range in colour from purplish brown to green. A native of western North America, from Oregon south to southern California and Mexico. In Europe, it is a rather scarce ornamental tree and is grown occasionally for its timber.

Beautiful Fir *Abies amabilis* Up to 30m or more

As its name suggests, this tall tree has a pleasing shape when seen in mature collections. The needles are 25mm long, stiff and rather flattened. They are blunt-tipped, deep green in colour and give off a smell of citrus when bruised. Cones are 10 to 12cm long and rather elongated egg-shaped in outline; they become deep purplish brown in colour with maturity. A native of north-western North America from south-east Alaska to Washington State and Oregon. In Europe, it is grown occasionally in ornamental collections.

St Lucia Fir *Abies bracteata* Up to 35m or more

An elegant and stately tree when seen in mature ornamental collections. The needles are 50m long and rather stiff. They are dark green in colour, sharply pointed at the tip and narrowly waisted at the base. The highly distinctive cones are 9cm long, egg-shaped in outline and carry extremely long bracts, sometimes up to 6cm in length. This attractive fir is a native of the hills and mountains of the same name in California. In Europe, it is seen mostly in ornamental collections.

Norway Spruce *Picea abies* subsp. *abies* Up to 65m

Well known as the popular 'Christmas Tree' this distinctly conical evergreen has characteristically curved branches, the upper ones ascending, the lower ones drooping. The bark is reddish-brown and smooth but develops cracks with age. Dark green needles are 10 to 25mm long and spread out and up to reveal the lower side of the shoot. The male cones are crimson. The female cones are cigar-shaped, 10 to 18cm long and dark red and erect at first, but ripening red-brown and becoming pendulous. A major forest tree in northern Europe and mountains further south.

Oriental Spruce *Picea orientalis* Up to 40m or more

A tall and sometimes straggly tree, rather similar to Norway spruce but with smaller needles. The twigs are densely hairy and the needles, the smallest of any spruce, are only 6 to 10mm long. These have rounded tips and are crowded and loosely pressed to the shoot. The pendulous cones are 6 to 9cm long and are tapered at both ends. They are slightly curved and have broad, rounded scales. A native of south-western Asia, it is grown for timber in parts of Europe, mainly Austria, Belgium and Italy, and is also planted in gardens.

Serbian Spruce *Picea omrika* Up to 30m

This distinctively slender evergreen has a spire-like crown of blue-green foliage. Red-brown bark falls away in flakes. Twigs are densely hairy with woody, peg-like leaf bases. Flattened needles are 8 to 18mm long with two broad, whitish bands beneath. Upper needles are pressed forward on the shoot while the lower ones spread out to leave a parting below the shoot. Crimson cones ripen brown and reach 3 to 6cm in length. Native only to the Drina River Basin in former Yugoslavia. It is planted for timber in parts of Scandinavia and widely grown as an ornamental tree.

Brewer's Weeping Spruce *Picea breweriana* 10 to 20m

This unusual and attractive evergreen produces sheets of blackish-green, weeping foliage which hangs vertically from the upswept or spreading branches. The bark is smooth and breaks into scales. Slender twigs are finely hairy. The stiff, fleshy needles are 20 to 35mm long and are flattened and curved. These spread out all around the shoot and are dark bluish-green with two white bands beneath. The narrow, cylindrical cones are 10 to 12mm long and purple ripening to brown. Native only to mountains in California and Oregon. It is widely planted in European parks and gardens.

19

Sitka Spruce *Picea sitchensis* Up to 60m

This vigorous and fast-growing evergreen has bluish foliage and grey bark that peels into thin scales or plates. The main branches are ascending or level with flattened, stiff and pointed needles 15 to 30mm long. These are dark green above, with two bluish-white bands beneath, and radiate around the shoot at first. Later, the upper ones become pressed to the shoot while the lower ones spread to leave a parting. Mature cones are 6 to 10cm long, pendulous and bluntly cigar-shaped. Native to western North America and is widely planted for timber in north-western Europe.

Colorado Blue Spruce *Picea pungens* Up to 30m

This distinctly conical evergreen has a narrowly conical crown with regular whorls of branches held horizontally. The bark is dark brown and scaly. The yellow-brown twigs are rough with peg-like leaf bases. Stiff and prickly needles are usually grey-green; sometimes blue. Needles are four-sided, 20 to 30mm long and spread out around the shoot before curving up and forwards. Mature cones are 6 to 10cm long, pendulous and are broadly cylindrical. Native to western North America and is planted for timber on drier soils in northern and central parts of Europe. Blue-leaved forms are grown for show.

Western Hemlock-spruce *Tsuga heterophylla* Up to 70m

This graceful evergreen has drooping tips to the branches and leading shoot. Irregular whorls of branches clothe the trunk almost to the ground. Grey bark becomes purple-brown and flaking. Young twigs have long hairs. Blunt, flattened needles vary from 6 to 20mm in length and are dark green above with two broad white bands below. The cushion-like bases persist after the needles fall. Male cones are red, female cones are red-brown, 2 to 2.5cm long and drooping ovoid to cylindrical. Native to the west coast of North America and grown for timber in northern Europe.

Eastern Hemlock-spruce *Tsuga canadensis* Up to 30m

Superficially similar to western hemlock-spruce but with a much broader, bushier crown. Bark is purple-grey and ridged. Needles are 8 to 18mm long, dark green with two narrow white bands below; they have rounded tips. The central row of needles on the upper side of the shoot is twisted, clearly showing the pale underside. Ripe female cones are 1.5 to 2cm in length and hang from short stalks. Native to the east coast of North America. In Europe, it is occasionally planted for timber but is more commonly seen as an ornamental tree.

21

Douglas-fir *Pseudotsuga menziesii* Up to 55m

An extremely tall evergreen which seldom reaches its maximum height of 100m in Europe. The crown is conical with irregular whorls of branches. Rigid, corky bark becomes grey or dark purplish-brown with age. Hairy twigs bear projecting elliptical scars of fallen needles. Needles are 20 to 35mm long, narrow and sharp-pointed but otherwise soft and dark green above with two white bands below. They mostly spread to leave partings on both sides. Cones are 5 to 10cm long, ovoid and pendulous, with three-pronged bracts protruding beyond the cone-scales. Native to western North America and extensively planted in Europe.

Bosnian Pine *Pinus leucodermis* Up to 30m

The pyramidal crown of this stout pine is dense and regular with down-curved branches. The smooth grey bark cracks to reveal yellowish patches. The glabrous twigs have an ash-grey bloom. Paired blackish-green needles are 70 to 90mm long, stiff and sharp-pointed. These cover the shoot densely except at the base of the current year's growth which is bare for a short way leaving a cup-shaped tuft of needles at the tip. The cones are 7 to 8cm long, ovoid and slightly shiny, ripening from blue-brown in the second year. It is a native of Italy and the Balkans.

Pinus heldreichii Up to 20m

This short and stout pine is similar in many respects to Bosnian Pine except for its more rounded crown. The smooth grey bark cracks to reveal yellowish patches and the twigs are glabrous. The twigs retain their ash-grey bloom for the first year only, turning brown in the second year of growth. The paired needles are 60 to 90mm long and are brighter green than Bosnian pine. When mature, the cones are pale brown and the exposed ends of the cone-scales are flat with a straight spine. Native to mountains in the central Balkan peninsula.

Austrian Pine *Pinus nigra* subsp. *nigra* Up to 50m

The dense, hard and rough foliage gives this tall evergreen a dark overall appearance. Young specimens are pyramidal, old ones are flat-topped. Bark is grey-brown to black and very rough. The yellowish-brown twigs are rough with persistent leaf-bases. Dark green needles are 100 to 150mm long and grow in pairs on the twigs; they are toothed and thickened at the tips. Cones are 5 to 8cm long, paired, ripening from pink to pale, shiny brown. Found on alkaline and neutral soils in central and coastal southern Europe and is also widely planted.

23

Corsican Pine *Pinus nigra* subsp. *laricio* Up to 40m or more

This rather straggly evergreen is similar to its close relative Austrian pine but with fewer, shorter branches and sparser foliage. Bark is greyish-brown to dark brown and rather rough. The slender, grey-green needles are soft and flexible, and often twisted in young trees; they are 120 to 170mm long and grow in pairs grouped in whorls along the twigs. Cones are 5 to 8cm long and are usually seen in pairs or clusters. Native to southern parts of Europe, growing on poor soils. It is widely planted for timber, also being used to stabilise sand dunes in some areas.

Crimean Pine *Pinus nigra* subsp. *carmanica* Up to 30m

A distinctive evergreen with the main trunk dividing 5 to 10m from the ground. The foliage is similar in overall appearance to that of Cosican pine but is often rather sparse on the lower half of the tree. The bark is grey-brown and rough. The slender, grey-green needles are 100 to 130mm long and grow in pairs, arranged in whorls along the twigs. The cones are 6 to 10cm long and are usually seen in pairs. Crimean Pine is native to Crimea, the Caucasus, the Balkans and Asia Minor. In Europe, it is seen mainly in tree collections.

Scots Pine *Pinus sylvestris* Up to 35m

A familiar evergreen, often with a small, flat and lop-sided crown. Young trees are conical with whorled branches while older trees have bare lower trunks revealing conspicuous reddish, fissured bark lower down and papery bark higher up. The paired grey or bluish-green needles are 25 to 80mm long and twisted and finely toothed with a long, greyish sheath around the base of each pair. Male cones are yellow or red. Female cones are short-stalked and are seen in clusters of one to three, each 2 to 8cm long; they are ovoid to conical. Scots Pine is a common forest-forming tree on poor, light soils or high ground throughout Europe.

Dwarf Mountain Pine *Pinus mugo* Up to 3m, rarely more

This shrubby, upland pine generally hugs the ground but can form a conical tree. It is an evergreen tree or shrub with numerous crooked, spreading stems and branches. Twigs are initially green but become brown. Paired needles are 30 to 80 × 1.5 to 2mm, bright green, stiff and curved. The ovoid cones are 2 to 5cm long and occur in clusters of one to three. The exposed end of each scale is usually flat with a small spine. Native to high mountain slopes in central Europe and the Balkans and is planted elsewhere to stabilise sand or as an avalanche break.

Mountain Pine *Pinus uncinata* Up to 25m

This upland species is similar to, but much taller than, dwarf mountain pine but is sometimes included in that species. Tree is usually upright and borne on a single trunk. The bark is grey and scaly and the twigs are initially green but become brown with age. Paired needles are 30 to 80mm long and are bright green, stiff and curved. The mature cones are 5 to 7cm long with the exposed ends of the cone-scales, especially the lower ones, hooked or curved downwards. A mountain species that is found in the Alps, the Pyrenees and mountains of central Spain.

Maritime Pine *Pinus pinaster* Up to 40m

Mature specimens of this evergreen conifer have a long, bare trunk and an open crown of wide-spreading branches bearing long, stiff needles. Bark is red-brown, deeply fissured; twigs are reddish-brown. Greyish-green needles grow in pairs, 100 to 250 × 2mm. Young female cones are pink and seen in clusters of three to five at the tips of the shoots. Mature cones are 8 to 22cm, pale brown and oval. They ripen in the second year and persist on the tree. This pine grows on sandy soils around the Mediterranean and is planted elsewhere for timber and shelter.

Aleppo Pine *Pinus halepensis* Up to 20m

Bright, shiny green foliage distinguishes this drought-resistant conifer. Branches are twisted and sparse. Trunk is stout and also twisted. Bark is pale grey, becoming reddish-brown, fissured and flaking. First year twigs are grey while older ones are brown. The paired, clear green needles are 60 to 150 × 0.7mm, stiff, curved and spine-tipped. The reddish-brown cones are 5 to 12cm long, are borne on thick, scaly, recurved stalks and ripen in the second year. The seeds have a 20mm long wing. It is common in parts of the Mediterranean, and is often planted as a wind break.

Monterey Pine *Pinus radiata* Up to 40m

This high-domed conifer has spreading lower branches that sometimes reach to the ground. Bark is thick, dark brown and deeply ridged in old trees; twigs are glabrous and reddish-brown. Slender, bright green needles are 100 to 150mm long, borne in threes and densely crowded on the shoots. Cones 7 to 14cm long, ovoid and asymmetric at the base; they are borne in clusters of three to five and ripen shiny brown. Cones remain closed on the tree for many years. Native to Monterey County in California and is grown for timber and shelter in Europe.

27

Canary Island Pine *Pinus canariensis* Up to 30m

This slightly weeping evergreen has spreading branches with pendulous twigs which are prominently ridged yellow. Pointed needles are 200 to 300mm long, borne in threes and are densely crowded on the shoot. The solitary or clustered cones are 10 to 20cm long, ovoid to conical and bent back on a short stalk when mature. The exposed ends of the cone-scales are pyramidal with a central dimple. This species of pine is endemic to the Canary Islands and although once widespread there is now much reduced. It is planted for timber in Mediterranean countries, principally Italy.

Western Yellow Pine *Pinus ponderosa* Up to 75m

This is the tallest pine commonly planted in Europe. The crown is conical with drooping branches upturned at the tip. Trunk is stout with thick, yellowish reddish-brown bark. Twigs are glabrous, orange-brown or green turning nearly black with age. Curved, aromatic needles are 100 to 250mm long and are borne in threes, rarely in pairs or fives. The solitary or clustered, ovoid cones are 8 to 15cm long, ripen reddish-brown and spread away from the shoot or turn downwards. Native to western North America and is planted in Europe for timber and, more commonly, for ornament.

Weymouth Pine *Pinus strobus* Up to 50m

This evergreen is broadly pyramidal when it is mature. Bark of young trees is greyish-green; brown and fissured in mature trees. Young shoots have tufts of reddish-brown. Flexible, bluish-green needles are 50 to 140mm long and arranged in horizontally held bundles of five with a distinctive tuft of hairs at the base of the bundle-sheath. Pendulous, sticky female cones are 8 to 20cm long and cylindrical. They ripen in the second year and the seeds have a wing that is 18 to 25mm wide. A native of North America which is now planted on a wide scale, particularly in Europe, as a timber tree.

Calabrian Pine *Pinus brutia* Up to 20m

A robust evergreen conifer with branches that are often twisting. Bark is shiny and smooth, ash-grey at first but becoming reddish-brown and fissured in mature specimens. Twigs are glabrous, greyish at first but becoming green. The needles are dark green, often slightly curved, 9 to 12mm long and borne in pairs. The cones are 6 to 12cm long, ovoid and are borne singly or in clusters of two or three. A drought-resistant species that grows in hot, dry regions of Calabria, Turkey and Crete. It is occasionally grown in collections.

29

Bristle-cone Pine *Pinus aristata* Up to 15m

This small tree or sprawling shrub has a short trunk with thin, smooth bark becoming ridged and scaly with age. Twigs are yellowish-brown with minute reddish hairs. The stiff pointed needles are 20 to 40mm long, borne in fives and densely crowded. They are deep green with conspicuous white dots of resin and smell of turpentine when they are crushed. Cones are 4 to 9cm long, cylindrical and ripen in the second year. Each cone scale is tipped with a long, slender spine. Native to high altitudes in the Rocky Mountains and planted on a small scale for timber in Europe. Usually found in private collections.

Bhutan Pine *Pinus wallichiana* Up to 50m

An elegant evergreen with an open crown of wide-spreading, drooping branches. Bark is smooth or shallowly fissured and grey-brown. The twigs are grey-green with a purplish waxy bloom when young, that darkens with age. The flexible, grey-green needles are 80 to 200mm long, sharp-pointed, toothed and borne in fives. Cones are 15 to 25cm long, solitary or in clusters and cylindrical; they are pendulous, pale brown and resinous when ripe. Native to cool zones in the Himalayas. It is pollution-resistant and is planted for timber in Italy, elsewhere in Europe for ornament.

Arolla Pine *Pinus cembra* 25 to 40m

This densely foliaged pine retains its level branches so that the trunk is almost completely hidden. Scaly bark is marked with resinous blisters and the twigs are covered with brownish-orange hair. Stiff, shiny green needles are 50 to 80mm long, grouped in erect bundles of five and crowded on the twigs. Male cones are purple or yellow. Female cones are 5 to 6cm long, ovoid and ripening from bluish-purplish to brown. Cone scales are rounded and tipped with minute hairs. Native to the Alps and Carpathians at altitudes of 1500 to 2400m. It is often planted for timber in northern Europe.

European Larch *Larix decidua* Up to 35m

The needles of this deciduous conifer turn yellow in autumn. Bark is grey to pale brown, becoming thick before cracking away. Pendulous twigs are yellowish, knotted and roughened with old leaf bases. Long shoots bear scattered needles while short spur-like shoots bear needles in tufts of 30 to 40. Flattened needles are 12 to 30mm long, soft and pale green. Young cones appear just before the leaves: males yellow, females red. Mature cones are 2 to 3cm long and ovoid; persisting after shedding seeds. Native to the Alps and Carpathians but is widely planted for timber in Europe.

31

Japanese Larch *Larix kaempferi* Up to 40m

Similar to European larch but with a distinct blue-green tone to the foliage. The upper part of trunk may twist spirally, especially in young trees. The crown is broader than that of European larch with wide-spreading branches and waxy orange twigs. Bark is reddish-brown. The needles have two distinct white bands beneath. Young female cones are creamy yellow. Mature cones are 1.5 to 3.5cm long with softly hairy scales, the upper edges of which curve outwards. Native to Japan and an important timber tree in much of northern Europe including Britain.

Hybrid Larch *Larix × eurolepis* Up to 35m

This vigorous deciduous conifer is a hybrid between European and Japanese larches and has features intermediate between both parents. In some areas it merges with European larch in terms of features and appearance. The bark is grey-brown or reddish and the shoots are waxy and yellow-brown. The needles are grey-green, usually pointed and 50mm long; they are carried in clusters of 30 to 40. The mature cones are 2 to 3.5cm long with rounded, slightly reflexed scales. This species is planted for timber and as windbreaks in various parts of Europe.

Deodar *Cedrus deodara* Up to 60m

The stout trunk of this stately evergreen supports a triangular crown with downswept branches and a drooping leading shoot. Twigs are densely hairy and the shoots are long or short and spur-like. Pale green needles 20 to 50mm long are three-sided and scattered along the long shoots; on the short shoots they are borne in rosette-like tufts of 15 to 20. Cones are large and erect; males 5 to 12cm, yellow, female cones, 8 to 12cm. Native to the Himalayas. In Europe it is planted for timber in the south and grown for ornament elsewhere.

Atlantic Cedar *Cedrus atlantica* up to 40m

This tall, loosely conical evergreen is similar to Deodar but with upwardly angled branches and a stiff, erect leading shoot. The young twigs are downy. Needles are 10 to 30mm long and are usually green but occasionally blue-green; they are carried in tufts of 10 to 45 on short shoots. Male cones are 3 to 5cm long while female cones are 5 to 8cm long and have a flat or dimpled top and ripen in the second year. Native to the Atlas Mountains of North Africa. It is planted for timber in southern Europe and grown for ornament elsewhere especially the blue-leaved forms which are particularly attractive.

33

Cedar-of-Lebanon *Cedrus libani* Up to 40m

This tree is magnificent when mature. The young specimens are conical but the old tree develops a massive trunk and characteristic large, level branches with flat, shelf-like sprays of foliage. Twigs are glabrous. The dark green needles form tufts of 10 to 15 which are 20 to 30mm long. The barrel-shaped ripe cones are 7 to 12cm long and have rounded tops and ripen from purple-brown in the second year. Native to Turkey, Syria and the Lebanon. It is used for timber in Europe but, because it is slow-growing, is mainly seen as a park tree.

Swamp Cypress *Taxodium distichum* Up to 50m

As its name suggests, this deciduous conifer flourishes in water-logged soils. Stump-like breathing roots project up to 1m above ground around the base of its fluted trunk. Terminal shoots are short and persistant; side shoots are alternate and deciduous. Needles are 8 to 20mm long, flattened, pointed and pale green; they are borne spirally on the terminal shoots. Tiny male cones are seen in clusters while the thick-stalked female cones are 12 to 30mm long, globular and ripen from green-purple. Native to swamps in south-eastern North America. In Europe, it is planted for ornament and timber.

Pond Cypress *Taxodium ascendens* Up to 15m

A narrowly conical, deciduous conifer with a trunk which is rather fluted towards the base. Bark is reddish-brown and fissured. Needles are 10mm long, green and slightly flattened; they grow tightly pressed against the deciduous shoots which are shed in the autumn. Terminal shoots are branched and persistant. The male cones are greenish-yellow while the female cones are green ripening to brown and 2 to 3cm long. Native to swampy ground in south-east North America. In Europe, it is grown mainly as an ornamental tree.

Umbrella Pine *Sciadopitys verticillata* Up to 20m

This umbrella-shaped evergreen conifer is narrowly conicle. The trunk is often rather broad-based and the bark is reddish-brown and peels into long strips, especially near the base. Needles are 10 to 12mm long with a dark green upper surface and paler under surface. The male cones are yellowish and are carried in clusters while the female cones are green, ripening to deep reddish-brown; when mature they are ovoid and 6 to 8cm long. Native to upland regions of Japan. In Europe, it is grown occasionally as an ornamental tree.

35

Dawn Redwood *Metasequoia glyptostroboides* Up to 40m

The bark of this deciduous conifer is typically reddish-brown and peels into flaky strips. The side shoots and needles are arranged in pairs. The needles themselves are 20 to 25mm long, flattened and become dark green with maturity. The male cones are yellowish and are clustered around the leaf bases. The female cones are greenish at first but ripen brown; the cone-scales lack spines. Dawn redwood was previously known only from fossils until it was discovered as a living tree in China in 1941. It is now fairly frequently planted in European parks and gardens for ornament.

Coast Redwood *Sequoia sempervirens* Up to 112m

Well known as the tallest tree in the world, this evergreen conifer has a large trunk clad with very soft and thick, fibrous reddish bark. The lower branches are angled downward. Needles on the leading and cone-bearing shoots are 6mm long, scale like and spirally arranged; those on the paired side shoots are 6 to 20mm long, flattened, pointed and curved. Ovoid cones are 1.8 to 2.5 × 1.2cm. Each of the 15 to 20 cone scales has a sunken centre. Native to the Pacific coast of North America and is planted mainly for ornament in western Europe.

Wellingtonia *Sequoiadendron giganteum* Up to 90m

This massive evergreen conifer has a trunk up to 7m in diameter, even when measured above the thickly buttressed base. It is a narrowly conical tree with downswept branches turning up at their tips. Bark is spongy and red-brown. Scale-like needles are 4 to 10mm long, spirally arranged and pressed against the shoot. Cones, 5 to 8 × 3 to 4.5mm, ovoid and blunt. Each of the 25 to 40 cone scales has a sunken centre and often a spine. Native to the Sierra Nevada mountains of California. In Europe, it is grown mainly for ornament.

Japanese Red Cedar *Cryptomeria japonica* Up to 35m

This narrowly conical evergreen has irregularly whorled branches and shoots hidden by awl-shaped needles. Bark is pale red, soft and thick. Sparsely branched green twigs often droop; bright green needles are 6 to 15mm long and spirally arranged on the shoot. Orange male cones are clustered at the tips of the shoots. Female cones, 1.2 to 3cm long when ripe and borne on stout side-shoots. Each of the 20 to 30 cone-scales has five hooked spines in the centre. Native to China and Japan. In Europe, it is grown mainly for ornament and occasionally for timber.

Monkey Puzzle *Araucaria araucana* Up to 25m

This easily recognisable tree has whorls of stiff and intricate branches. Leaves are 30 to 40mm long, broadly triangular, rigid and sharp-pointed and arranged in close-set, overlapping whorls which completely hide the shoot. Leaves remain green for 10 to 15 years. Male and female cones are borne on different trees. Males are brown, 10cm long and form clusters at the tips of the shoots; females are globular, solitary, 10 to 17cm long, with golden-tipped scales. Native to coastal mountains of Chile and Argentina. It is planted in western Europe for ornament.

Norfolk Island Pine *Araucaria heterophylla*

This species is very unusual and distinctive. The sparse, spreading branches are arranged at intervals up the trunk, right from ground level, and are topped by a rounded and layered crown. The soft leaves are narrow and pointed; when young they are spreading but, as the tree ages, they become pressed against the shoot. The foliage of mature trees has a passing resemblence to the fronds of palms. As its name suggests, it is native only to Norfolk Island in the north of New Zealand. It is a popular ornamental tree in Mediterranean countries.

Western Red Cedar *Thuja plicata* Up to 65m

This erect evergreen is pyramidal or conical. The trunk is stout and often fluted, with reddish, shredding bark. The leading shoot and resin-scented foliage never droop; instead, the latter form flattened sprays. Leaves are 2 to 3mm long, glossy green above and faintly marked with white below. They are pressed against the shoot in alternating pairs, the lateral pairs larger than the vertical pairs. Female cones are ovoid, 12mm long, ripening green-brown. They have 10 to 12 leafy, overlapping cone-scales. Native to western North America and is planted in cool, damps parts of western and central Europe.

White Cedar *Thuja occidentalis* up to 15m

A narrowly conical, evergreen conifer. The trunk is not as stout as western red cedar and the bark is reddish-brown, peeling into long strips. Foliage is resin-scented and carried in flattened sprays. Scale-like leaves are 2 to 3mm long, green above and paler below with no white markings. Male cones are reddish while female cones ripen from green-brown, are 10 to 12mm long, with 8 to 10 leafy and overlapping cone-scales. Native to mountainous regions of North America. In Europe, it is widely planted for ornament and appears in a variety of cultivars.

Hiba *Thujopsis dolabrata* Up to 18m

Hiba *Thujopsis dolabrata* Up to 18m

This rather attractive evergreen is usually broadly conical. The trunk often divides and branches low down and the bark is reddish-brown, shredding into vertical strips. The scale-like leaves are 4 to 7mm long, opposite, with a dark green upper surface and white markings on the underside. The foliage is aromatic and is carried in flattened sprays. Male cones are blackish; female cones are brown, 1.2 to 1.5cm long with 6 to 8 cone-scales. Native to mountainous regions in Japan. In Europe, it is widely planted as an ornamental tree.

Hinoki Cypress *Chamaecyparis obtusa* Up to 35m

Rather similar to the more widespread Lawson Cypress this broadly conical evergreen has reddish bark which peels in long strips. Flattened sprays of foliage give a sweet, resinous scent when crushed. The scale-like leaves are 2mm long and closely pressed to the shoot; they are blunt, not pointed, and have X- or Y-shaped white markings on those beneath the shoot. Male cones are blackish-red, female cones are bluish-green, 8mm in diameter, globular and made up of eight scales. Native to Japan and is commonly planted in Europe for ornament.

Lawson Cypress *Chamaecyparis lawsoniana* Up to 45m

Pendulous sprays of foliage and a nodding leading shoot give the whole tree a drooping appearance. Dark grey-brown bark cracks into plates. The parsley- scented light green shoots form flattened, pendulous sprays. Alternating pairs of 2mm long, scale-like leaves are closely pressed against the shoot; upper leaves are dark green while those on the lower side have whitish marks. Male cones are blackish-red while female cones are bluish-green, 8mm in diameter, globular and made up of eight scales which touch edge-to-edge. This species is native to western North America and widely planted in Europe for ornament, shelter and timber.

Leyland Cypress × *Chamaecyparis leylandii* Up to 35m

A vigorous hybrid between Nootka and Monterey cypresses. Produces a narrow, columnar crown with dense, upwardly angle branches from base to tip. The leading shoot leans but does not droop. Foliage sprays may be flattened or not depending on the form. Scaly leaves are 0.5 to 2mm long, dark green above and yellowish beneath, growing in alternating pairs. Female cones are globular, green when young, 2 to 3cm long and brown and woody when ripe. Commonly planted for hedges and gardens. Other forms are cv. 'Hagerston Grey' with grey leaves and cv. 'Leighton Green' with green leaves.

Sawara Cypress *Chamaecyparis pisifera* Up to 40m

A broadly or narrowly conical, evergreen tree. Bark is reddish-brown, ridged and cracked and often peels slightly. The aromatic foliage is carried in flattened sprays and the scale-like, pointed leaves are arranged in pairs which alternate along the stem; the leaves themselves are 0.5 to 2mm long, dark green above and with white markings on the under surface. The cones are rounded and pea-like, 7 to 9mm in diameter and ripen from green to brown. A native of upland regions in Japan. In Europe, it is frequently planted in parks and gardens for ornament.

Nootka Cypress *Chamaecyparis nootkaensis* Up to 40m

This narrowly conical evergreen tree has reddish- or greyish- brown bark, rather shaggy, which often peels into thin strips. The foliage forms drooping, flattened sprays which have an aromatic and rather unpleasant odour when rubbed. The scale-like leaves are pointed, dark green above and pale green beneath without any white markings. The female cones are rounded, 10mm in diameter, and the cone-scales have curved spines. Native of coastal north-west North America. In Europe, it is grown occasionally for ornament.

Monterey Cypress *Cupressus macrocarpa* Up to 35m

Upswept branches distinguish this evergreen conifer. The foliage is cord-like and the crown is narrow and pointed when young but broadly domed or flat-topped in old trees. Bark is ridged and yellowish-brown. The blunt, scaly leaves are 1 to 2mm long and are closely pressed against the shoot in alternating and overlapping pairs. Cones are borne at the shoot tips; males 3 to 5mm long and yellow, females are 20 to 30mm long, globose to ellipsoid. The 8 to 14 cone-scales meet edge to edge. Native to southern California. In Europe, it is grown for ornament and shelter.

Italian Cypress *Cupressus sempervirens* Up to 30m

In the wild, these sombre evergreen trees are low-growing with spreading branches; cultivars often form dense, spire-like trees, the upswept branches giving a characteristic narrowly columnar crown. Bark is greyish, often with spiral ridges. Blunt leaves are 0.5 to 1mm long, dark green and pressed against the shoot in alternating pairs. Cones are ellipsoid to oblong, 2.5 to 4cm in diameter and have 8 to 14 scales that meet edge to edge; each scale has a blunt, central point and wavy margins. Native to the Aegean region but long cultivated in southern Europe, especially Italy, and is frequently naturalised.

43

Incense Cedar *Calocedrus decurrens* Up to 35m

A tall and narrowly columnar, evergreen tree with a characteristically rounded top. The bark is reddish-brown and the foliage is highly aromatic, smelling of incense. The leaves are arranged in whorls of four; they are sharp-tipped and lie pressed tightly against the stems. The male cones are yellow and 3 to 6mm in diameter. The female cones are 2 to 3cm in diameter, ovoid and pointed; they are borne at the end of stems and the seeds have wings. A native of eastern North America which is occasionally grown in Europe, mainly for ornament.

Juniper *Juniperus communis* Up to 6m

This small tree is often no more than a low shrub. Bark is reddish and shredding, twigs are slender and angled. Needle-like leaves are 8 to 30mm long and arranged in whorls of three. They are stiff, prickly and bluish with a broad white band above. Male and female cones are borne on different trees. Males are small and yellowish. Females are oval to globular, 6 to 9mm long, ripening from green to blue-black in the second or third year. Juniper is found scattered throughout Europe, especially on lime-rich soils. In southern Europe it grows mainly on mountains.

Phoenician Juniper *Juniperus phoenicea* Up to 8m

This small evergreen tree is sometimes no more than a spreading shrub. The foliage can be either cord-like shoots with scaly leaves or young growth bearing needles. Twigs are round in cross-section. The needle-like, young growth leaves are up to 14mm long and wide-spreading in whorls of three. Adult leaves are 1mm long, blunt with pale margins and closely pressed to the shoots. Female cones are 6 to 14mm long, blackish at first but becoming green, then yellow and finally ripening dark red in the second year. Widespread throughout coastal regions of the Mediterranean.

Pencil Cedar *Juniperus virginiana* Up to 30m

The tallest juniper commonly seen in Europe, it has a narrowly pyramidal and spire-like crown. The crushed foliage has an unpleasant smell and the twigs are four-angled in cross-section. Adult leaves are 0.5 to 1mm long, needle-like juvenile leaves are 5 to 6mm long with two white bands below. Both types of leaves are borne in alternating pairs. Female cones are 4 to 6mm long, ovoid and ripen from bluish-green to brownish-violet in the second year. Native to North America. In Europe, it is planted for timber and is also frequently planted in gardens and parks for ornament.

Chinese Juniper *Juniperus chinensis* Up to 15m

A narrowly conical, evergreen tree with rounded twigs. The needle-like juvenile leaves are 6 to 8mm long, sharply pointed and banded white above; they are borne in whorls of three. The scale-like adult leaves are 1 to 1.5mm long with all but the tips pressed close to the shoot. The male cones are yellow. The female cones are 6 to 8mm long, globose and ripen from bluish to brownish-violet in the second year. Native to China and Japan. In Europe, it is frequently planted in parks and gardens as an ornamental tree. There are many cultivated varieties.

Yew *Taxus baccata* Up to 25m

This evergreen tree or shrub has a thick trunk and rounded crown. Bark is reddish, flaking and peeling. Flattened, sharp-pointed needles are 10 to 30mm long, spirally arranged on the twig but spread out to form two lateral rows. They are dark dull green above and yellowish beneath. Male flowers, yellowish, and female flowers, greenish, are borne on different trees. Berry-like fruit consists of a seed 6 to 7mm long, surrounded by a fleshy, dull scarlet, cup-like structure - the aril - up to 1cm long. Yew is shade-tolerant and common across Europe, in woods and scrub.

California Nutmeg *Torreya californica* Up to 30m

This broadly conical, evergreen tree has whorls of horizontal branches. The broad-based trunk has greyish-brown, ridged bark. The foliage is heavily aromatic and the leaves are sharp-pointed and 50 to 60mm long; they are dark green above with pale bands on the under surface. Male and female flowers are usually borne on separate trees. Male flowers are buffish-yellow and appear in the leaf axils towards the ends of shoots while female flowers are small and green. The fruits comprise a single seed enclosed in a dark greenish aril, resembling a nutmeg. Native to California but widely planted.

Plum-fruited Yew *Podocarpus andinus* Up to 15m

This conical evergreen tree or large shrub usually has several trunks. Bark is smooth, dark brown, fading to grey with age; young twigs are green. Needles are up to 5cm long, spirally arranged but spreading to either side of the shoot to form two forward-pointing rows. They are narrow, flattened, straight or slightly curved, bright green above with a paler lower surface. Yellow male flowers and green female flowers usually occur on different trees. Fleshy fruits are 15 to 20mm long and yellowish. Native to southern Chile but planted in Europe for ornament and hedging.

47

Willow Podocarp *Podocarpus salignus* Up to 15m

As its name suggests, the leaves of this bushy evergreen shrub or tree resemble those of willows. It has lush, dense foliage and usually multiple trunks. Bark is reddish-brown, peeling into long strips in mature specimens. Young twigs are green. Leaves are narrow and up to 10cm in length with a soft, leathery quality. Male and female flowers are usually borne on separate trees. Male flowers are catkin-like clusters and females are greenish clusters. Native to Chile and is grown ornamentally in Europe, mainly for its foliage.

Totara *Podocarpus totara* Up to 15m

In European cultivation this species is large, evergreen shrub or a small tree, usually with a single trunk. Bark is greyish-brown to reddish-brown and peeling, and the young twigs are green. Leaves are tough, needle-shaped and yellowish-green in colour. Male and female flowers are usually borne on separate trees. Male flowers are catkin-like clusters and female flowers are greenish clusters. Native to New Zealand and is grown in Europe for ornament. It only thrives in the mildest of climates.

Maidenhair-tree *Ginkgo biloba* Up to 30m

This irregularly conical tree has one trunk or sometimes more. Leathery leaves, 12 × 10cm, are notched, fan-shaped with radiating veins. Long shoots have widely spaced leaves and the spur-like short shoots have clusters of leaves. Male and female flowers are borne on separate trees; males comprise thick, erect catkins and females occur singly or in pairs on long stalks. Fleshy, oval fruit is 2.5 to 3cm long, yellowish when ripe. Native to China but probably extinct in the wild. It is widely planted in Europe as an ornamental tree.

Almond Willow *Salix triandra* Up to 10m

The bark of this bushy tree or shrub is dark grey and flakes to reveal large reddish-brown patches. Twigs are olive-brown, glabrous, ridged or angled when young, becoming cylindrical with age. The alternate leaves are 4 to 11cm, long-pointed with a thickened, toothed margin; they are glabrous, dark dull green above and green to slightly bluish beneath. The short petiole has a pair of toothed, ear-shaped stipules at the base. The erect, yellow male catkins are 2.5 to 5cm long and appear on separate trees from smaller females. It is widespread in Europe except the far north.

Crack Willow *Salix fragilis* Up to 25m

This tree has a thick and leaning trunk and a broad, rounded crown. Twigs are glabrous and olive-brown, and easily break away from the point where they join branches. Alternate leaves are 9 to 15cm long, lance-shaped, long-pointed, hairy at first but soon glabrous and dark shiny green above and bluish-grey beneath. The similar-looking male and female catkins are 4 to 6cm long with short, hairy stalks; they are borne on different trees and appear with the leaves. Flowers during April and May and occurs on wet soils across most of lowland Europe.

White Willow *Salix alba* 10 to 25m

This attractive and distinctive tree has silvery-grey leaves, a well-defined trunk and upswept branches which usually form a narrow crown. Young twigs have silky hairs but later become glabrous and olive. The narrow, pointed leaves are 5 to 10cm long, alternate and silkily hairy at first with the upper surface later becoming dull green and naked. The erect, spreading catkins are borne on densely hairy stalks; they appear with the leaves, males and females on different trees. Males are cylindrical and 4 to 5cm long; females are shorter and greenish. Flowers during April and May, widespread in Europe.

Weeping Willow *Salix × chrysocoma* Up to 12m

The weeping branches of this beautiful tree form a broad, leafy dome. The twigs are slender, golden yellow, thinly hairy at first but soon becoming glabrous. The alternate, narrowly lanceolate and pointed leaves are 7 to 12cm long, and finely and evenly toothed. Young leaves are hairy but mature to become smooth, bright green above and bluish below. Male and female catkins grow on different trees and are borne on hairy stalks; they appear with the leaves. This hybrid tree is the commonest of several willows that weep and that are planted for ornament.

Grey Sallow *Salix cinerea* Up to 10m

A small tree or tall shrub with both leaves and young twigs felted with grey hairs. The crown is broad with spreading branches and the twigs become glabrous. Alternate leaves are 2 to 16cm long, and usually broadly oval with inrolled margins. There are ear-shaped stipules at the base of the petiole and short hairs on the dull green upper leaf surface. Stalkless male and female catkins appear on different trees before the leaves; they are erect, 2 to 3cm long and cylindrical to oval. Flowers during March and April and is common in wet habitats in most of Europe.

51

Goat Willow *Salix caprea* Up to 10m

This small tree or tall shrub has an open, spreading crown. The thick, stiff twigs are thinly hairy when young but become glabrous and yellowish. Peeled twigs are smooth and round. Alternate leaves are 5 to 12cm long, broadly oval to almost circular and shortly pointed. Leaves are dull green and hairy above and grey-woolly below; the petiole sometimes has two small, ear-shaped stipules at the base. Male and female catkins are borne on separate trees; they are 1.5 to 2.5cm long, erect, ovoid, stalkless and silvery-grey. Flowers in March and April and is common throughout Europe.

Osier *Salix viminalis* 3 to 6m

Typically cropped to provide a 'head' of long, straight, pliant twigs. These are covered with dense grey hairs at first but later become glabrous and shiny olive or brown. Narrow, tapering leaves are 10 to 15cm long, alternate, dull green above and densely covered with silvery hairs below; the margins are often wavy and inrolled. Male and female catkins appear on different trees before the leaves, are 1.5 to 3cm long, erect or curved, ovoid and densely hairy; males yellowish, females brownish. Flowers from February to April and is native to much of lowland Europe but also planted.

White Poplar *Populus alba* Up to 20m or more

The trunk of this spreading tree is often leaning and suckering at the base. The grey bark is fissured. Twigs have dense white hairs for the first year and then become glabrous. Alternate leaves are 3 to 9cm long, irregularly lobed with a round petiole. Leaves dark green above, pure white below. Hairy catkins appear before the leaves, males and females on different trees. Males are 4 to 7cm long with purple anthers and females are 3 to 5cm long with greenish stigmas. Flowers from February to March and grows on damp soil. Native to south-eastern Europe but grown for ornament elsewhere.

Grey Poplar *Populus × canescens* Up to 30m or more

This tall, robust, hybrid tree shares similarities with its parents, White Poplar and Aspen. The grey bark has rows of black lenticels and the young twigs are densely hairy but become glabrous. The alternate leaves are 3 to 6cm long and almost circular with irregular, wavy-toothed margins and flattened petioles. The catkins are similar to aspen and appear well before the leaves. Flowers in March and is usually found growing in river valleys. It is native or introduced to much of Europe and male trees appear to be much more common than females.

Aspen *Populus tremula* Up to 20m

A pale looking tree, the light, fluttering motions of the leaves accentuated by the flashing of their pale undersides. Bark is smooth and greyish and the young twigs are thinly hairy but becoming glabrous and grey-brown. Alternate leaves are 1.5 to 8cm long, broadly oval to almost circular and bluntly toothed; the petiole is flattened. Catkins are 5 to 8cm long and appear before the leaves. Males and females occur on different trees, the former with reddish-purple anthers, the latter with pink stigmas. Flowers from February to March. Common throughout Europe on poor soils.

Black Poplar *Populus nigra* Up to 35m

This robust tree has a broad, rounded crown with burs and swellings on the trunk. The dull grey bark is coarsely fissured and the twigs are glabrous and shiny orange-brown. Alternate leaves are 5 to 10cm long, triangular to oval with fine, blunt teeth, and a lower surface only slightly paler than the upper; the petiole is flattened. The loose-flowered catkins are 3 to 5cm long; males with crimson anthers and females with greenish stigmas appear on different trees before the leaves. Flowers during March and April and is native and widespread in most of Europe.

54

Lombardy Poplar *Populus nigra* var. *italica* Up to 35m

A familiar species to travellers in the countryside. Frequently seen along roads and avenues this distinctive, spire-like variety of black poplar has strongly upswept branches which are almost vertical. Bark and twigs are identical to Black Poplar as is the size, shape and colour of the alternate leaves. The tree is, however, always male and the 3 to 5cm long catkins with crimson anthers appear well before the leaves. Flowers during March and April. Originally planted in Italy it is now one of the most widely planted columnar poplars in Europe.

Hybrid Black Poplar *Populus × canadensis* Up to 30m

This spreading or narrow tree is a hybrid between Black Poplar and North American Cottonwood. The trunk lacks swellings or burrs and the bark is greyish and coarsely fissured. The twigs are greenish or sometimes reddish. The alternate leaves resemble those of Black Poplar but are more sharply and distinctly toothed and fringed with short hairs. The catkins are similar to Black Poplar. Flowers in March and April. It is a fast-growing tree and the various clones are widely planted, mainly in central Europe but also in western and southern regions. It is also grown for timber.

Western Balsam Poplar *Populus trichocarpa* Up to 25m

A tall, pleasantly fragrant tree, sometimes rather columnar in outline and with a rounded, domed top. The bark is greyish and fissured, the twigs are greenish and the buds are resinous and aromatic. Alternate leaves have bases cut straight across and have gradually tapering tips and slightly toothed margins; they are green above and greyish-white below. Catkins are 3 to 5cm long; males are brownish and females are greenish. Native to the Pacific slopes of north-western North America. It is best known for its amazingly rapid growth and is sometimes planted in Europe for ornament.

Walnut *Juglans regia* Up to 30m

This familiar tree has a spreading crown. Trunk has smooth, grey bark that eventually becomes fissured; the twigs bear Y-shaped leaf-scars. Alternate leaves are pinnately divided into seven to nine entire leaflets, each 6 to 15cm long. The solitary male flowers are pendulous catkins, 5 to 15cm long on old wood; females are produced in spire-like clusters of two to five on new growth. The green fruit is 4 to 5cm long and contains an oval stone, the walnut. Flowers during May and June. Native to the Balkans and parts of Asia but has been widely planted for centuries.

Black Walnut *Juglans nigra* Up to 50m

This fast-growing tree has a domed crown and abundant foliage. Bark is black or brown and deeply fissured; the twigs bear Y-shaped leaf scars. Alternate leaves are pinnately divided into 15 to 23 leaflets, each 6 to 12cm long, oval to lance-shaped, pointed and irregularly fine-toothed. Male flowers are 5 to 15cm long catkins and the female flowers are spike-like clusters of five. The pear-shaped fruit is 3 to 5cm long, green and hairy, and contains an oval stone. Flowers during May and June. It is native to North America and planted for its timber in eastern Europe.

Caucasian Wingnut *Pterocarya fraxinifolia* Up to 30m

The trunk of this broad-crowned tree is often divided, with numerous suckers around the base. Grey bark is deeply fissured and the twigs are twisted. Alternate leaves are pinnately divided into 21 to 41 narrowly oval, pointed leaflets. All are unequal, toothed and overlap slightly; they are shiny green with hairs along the midrib. Catkins are solitary, many-flowered and pendent; yellowish males are 5 to 12cm long, green females are 10 to 15cm long, lengthening in fruit. The fruit is a green nut. Flowers in March and April. It is native to the Caucasus and widely planted in European parks.

Shagbark Hickory *Carya ovata* Up to 40m

This broad tree has few, widespreading branches. Grey bark peels, giving the trunk a shaggy appearance. Alternate leaves are pinnately divided into five or seven pointed leaflets, 10 to 20cm long. Male and female flowers occur on the same tree. Males catkins are in clusters of three or more; females are small, greenish spike-like clusters of two to ten. Fruit is 3 to 6cm long, globose, with a thick, yellowish husk splitting to release a white, stony seed. Flowers in April and May. It is native to North America and is occasionally planted in Europe for timber.

Alder *Alnus glutinosa* Up to 20m

The sticky young twigs of this broadly conical tree are covered in orange warts. Alternate leaves are bright green, 4 to 10cm long, rounded and doubly toothed. The five to eight pairs of veins have long yellow hairs in the axils. The flowers appear before the leaves. Male catkins are pendulous, 2 to 6cm long, purple but later yellow while females are ovoid, 1.5cm long and in stalked clusters of three to eight, purplish then green. Fruit is 1 to 3cm long, cone-like with narrowly-winged nutlets. Flowers during February and March. It is common in wet places throughout Europe.

Italian Alder *Alnus cordata* Up to 20m

The bark of this broadly conical tree is grey and fissured; the twigs are greyish and slightly downy. Alternate leaves are dark green, up to 10cm long, rounded and bluntly toothed. The paired veins have hairs in the axils of the under surface. Male and female flowers grow on the same tree, before the leaves appear. Male catkins are 6 to 8cm long, pendulous and yellow while female catkins are small, red and occur in clusters. Cone-like fruits are woody and green at first, turning brown. Native to southern Italy and Corsica; sometimes planted in southern areas.

Green Alder *Alnus viridis* Up to 5m

The twigs of this small tree or shrub are smooth and the winter buds are stalkless. Alternate leaves are sticky when young, roughly circular, 4 to 9cm long and sharply double-toothed margins and hairs in the vein to axils beneath. Flowers appear before the leaves. Male catkins are yellow, pendulous and 5 to 12cm long. Females occur in clusters of three to five, are 1cm long, initially green then reddish. Woody, cone-like fruits are 1.5cm long and contain broadly winged nutlets. Flowers in April and is a mountain species occurring mainly in central and eastern Europe.

Downy Birch *Betula pubescens* Up to 25m

The appearance of this small tree or shrub is variable with spreading branches and smooth, brown or grey bark. Young twigs lack any resin glands but are covered with downy white hairs. The alternate, oval leaves are up to 5.5cm long, irregular at the base, and with regularly, coarsely-toothed margins. Male catkins, 3 to 6cm long, appear at the tips of twigs in the winter. Female catkins are 1 to 4cm long and composed of scales with spreading lateral lobes. Flowers are produced in April and May. It is tolerant of wet soils and cold climates and is common in northern and central Europe.

Silver Birch *Betula pendula* Up to 30m

This elegant tree has a silvery-white bark which breaks into dark, rectangular plates at the base of the trunk in older specimens. Branches are pendulous towards the tips and the young twigs have resin glands. The alternate leaves are 2.5 to 5cm long, oval to triangular, with double-toothed margins. Clusters of two to four male catkins, 3 to 6cm long, droop from the twig tips. Females are axillary, 1.5 to 3.5cm long and made up of scales with downcurved lobes. Flowers in April and May. It is native to much of Europe and thrives on light, sandy soil. It is sometimes grown in gardens as an ornamental.

Paper-bark Birch *Betula papyrifera* Up to 27m

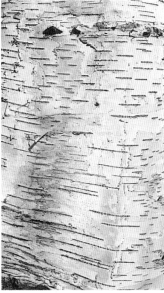

The distinctive bark of this unusual and attractive species gives it its common name. The bark peels into long paper-like strips; banded with rows of lenticels, usually white. Branches are strongly ascending and the twigs are rather hairy as well as warty. Leaves are similar to those of Silver Birch but 4 to 10cm long, more oval and longer pointed, thick and matt green. Male catkins are up to 10cm long and occur in clusters; females are axillary and 1.5 to 3.5cm long, the scales with erect lobes. Flowers from April to June. It is native to North America and is planted in European parks and gardens.

Hornbeam *Carpinus betulus* Up to 30m

Sizeable specimens of this species often have twisted or fluted trunks and branches. Bark is smooth, pale grey, sometimes fissured; the twigs are densely covered with hairs. Alternate leaves are 4 to 10cm long, sharply pointed and rounded at the base with sharply double-toothed margins. Pendulous yellow male catkins are up to 5cm long; green female catkins are 2cm, reaching 5 to 14cm long when in fruit. Each pair of nuts is attached to a three-lobed involucre up to 4cm long. Flowers during April and May. It is a common native hedgerow and woodland species in most of Europe.

61

Hazel *Corylus avellana* Up to 12m

The trunk of this small tree or shrub is short and the twigs have reddish, glandular hairs. Leaves are 10cm long, alternate and almost circular with a heart-shaped base and sharp, double-toothed margins. Flowers appear before the leaves; male catkins are up to 8cm long and bright yellow; the spike-like females are 5mm long and bright red. The nut is 1.5 to 2cm long and enveloped within a leafy, cup-like involucre. The edible kernel is the familiar hazelnut. It flowers from January to April. Native and common to most of Europe, especially in hedgerows.

Filbert *Corylus maxima* Up to 8m

A small tree or often only a shrub. The trunk is short and the twigs are covered in reddish, glandular hairs. Alternate leaves are stiffly hairy, 10cm long and almost circular in outline; they are heart-shaped at the base and have smoothly double-toothed margins. Flowers appear before the leaves; male catkins are up to 7cm long, pendulous and yellow; female catkins are spike-like with red styles. The hard-shelled nuts are solitary or in clusters and are completely enclosed by the involucre. Flowers in February and March. Native to the Balkans but widely planted and naturalised elsewhere.

Sweet Chestnut *Castanea sativa* Up to 30m

This well known tree has greyish, spirally fissured bark. Alternate leaves are 10 to 25cm long, narrowly oblong with a pointed tip, broadly wedge-shaped base and sharply-toothed margins. The slender, erect catkins have numerous yellowish male flowers in the upper part and females in groups of three towards the base. Each female cluster is surrounded by a green, spiky cupule which eventually splits to release one to three shiny, reddish-brown nuts. Flowers in June and July. It is native to southern Europe but widely planted elsewhere for its edible nuts.

Beech *Fagus sylvatica* Up to 40m

This species forms dense-canopied woods, the shade and deep leaf litter discouraging ground plants beneath. The crown is broadly domed, the bark is smooth and grey. Alternate, oval leaves are 4 to 9cm long with wavy margins. Flowers are yellowish; males occur in drooping, long-stalked heads with four to seven perianth lobes and paired female flowers are surrounded by a spiny, four -lobed involucre, 2 to 5cm in fruit, which eventually spreads to release two triangular brown nuts. Flowers in April and May. It is common in western and central Europe, typically on lime-rich soils.

63

Southern Beech *Nothofagus antarctica* Up to 15m

This smallish tree is broadly columnar in outline. The bark is shiny in young trees but, with maturity, becomes grey with cracks and fissures. Dark green, shiny leaves are oval, 3cm long, with wavy, finely-toothed margins. Small male flowers are seen in clusters of one to three and have reddish anthers; females are clustered in the leaf axils and have red stigmas and are up to 5mm long in fruit. A husk encloses three nuts. Flowers in February and March. Native to southern South America but is grown in European parks and gardens for ornament.

Dombey's Southern Beech *Nothofagus dombeyi* Up to 30m

A tall and broadly columnar tree, the bark of which is smooth in young trees but later becomes very dark grey with cracks and fissures. Leaves narrowly ovate, 5cm long, with finely-toothed margins; they are shiny and dark green above, and the under surface is suffused with black spots. Male flowers occur in clusters of three and the female flowers have red stigmas and grow in clusters of three; in fruit, they are 5mm long with a husk enclosing three nuts. Flowers in February and March. Native to southern Chile and Argentina. Grown for ornament in Europe.

Evergreen Oak *Quercus ilex* Up to 25m

This broadly-domed evergreen superficially resembles a holly tree. Bark is smooth, twigs are grey-brown and hairy. Alternate leaves are 3 to 7cm long, elliptical to oval, thick and leathery. Leaves are glossy green above and white- to green-felted below. Leaves are mostly entire but those on suckers may have wavy margins with short spiny teeth. Clusters of one to three acorns ripen in the first year; the cup is 12mm across with felted scales and encloses a third to a half of the acorn. Flowers in June. Native to the Mediterranean but widely planted for ornament elsewhere.

Kermes Oak *Quercus coccifera* Up to 5m

This small, densely-branched evergreen, closely resembles a holly bush. Young twigs are yellowish with star-shaped hairs. Alternate leaves are 1.5 to 4cm long, oval to oblong, sometimes heart-shaped at the base, and glossy; they are stiff and leathery with wavy and spine-toothed margins and a petiole only 1 to 4mm long. Acorns are usually solitary, ripening in the second year. The shallow acorn cups have stiff, spreading scales. Flowers in April and May. Native and widespread in much of the Mediterranean region, especially in the hotter, drier parts.

65

Cork Oak *Quercus suber* Up to 20m

The bark of this evergreen tree yields commercial cork. The thick, outer bark covers the thin, bright orange inner bark beneath. Alternate leaves are 3 to 7cm long, oblong-oval, dark green above and white-hairy below; the margins are wavy and toothed and the petiole is 8 to 15mm long. The acorns of early-flowering trees ripen in the first year. Acorn cup is 12 to 18mm in diameter and has long, spreading scales in the upper half and close-pressed scales in the lower. Flowers in May and June. Common in southern Europe and planted elsewhere for commercial cork.

Turkey Oak *Quercus cerris* Up to 35m

The dull, blackish bark of this spreading tree cracks into plates. The twigs are rough and brownish with short hairs. Variable leaves are alternate, 5 to 10cm long, oblong but tapering at both ends, with four to seven pairs of narrow lobes; they are rough and dull above and woolly below with a 8 to 15mm long petiole. The acorns are in clusters of one to five, ripening in the second year; half enclosed in 15 to 22mm diameter, woody cups with outward-curving scales. Flowers in May and June. Native to southern Europe except Spain and Portugal and is widely introduced elsewhere.

Sessile Oak *Quercus petraea* Up to 40m

The long trunk of this tree leads through to the top of the domed crown. Bark smooth and purplish-grey; twigs glabrous. Alternate leaves are 7 to 12cm long, widest above the middle, with five to eight pairs of rounded lobes; the petiole is 10 to 16mm long and the pale undersides have fine, close-pressed hairs and reddish tufts in the vein axils. Acorns are almost stalkless and are in clusters of one to six, ripening in the first year. The shallow cups are 12 to 18mm in diameter and have thin, downy scales. Flowers in May. Widespread in Europe except for parts of the Mediterranean.

Pedunculate Oak *Quercus robur* Up to 45m

This species is also known as English Oak. It is a massive tree which often dominates woodlands. Bark is dark grey; the young twigs are brownish and sometimes hairy. Alternate leaves are 10 to 12mm long, roughly oblong in outline with five to seven pairs of irregular lobes plus small ear-shaped projections at the base of the blade; the petiole is not more than 5mm long. The acorns are in clusters of one to five on 4 to 8mm long stalks and ripen in the first year. The scales of the 11 to 18mm diameter, shallow cups are fused except for their tips. Flowers in May and June. Common in most of Europe.

67

Hungarian Oak *Quercus frainetto* Up to 30m

This impressive domed tree has long, straight branches and a stout trunk. Bark is deeply fissured; the young twigs are downy at first, glabrous later. Alternate leaves, 10 to 20cm, are crowded towards the twig tips. They are deeply divided into seven to nine pairs of oblong lobes; there are two ear-shaped lobes at the base. The acorns are in clusters of two to five and ripen in the first year. The 6 to 12mm long cup encloses about a third of the acorn and has blunt, hairy scales that overlap. Flowers in May. It ranges from the Balkans to Hungary and southern Italy.

Red Oak *Quercus rubra* Up to 35m

The leaves of this tree turn a stunning scarlet in autumn, hence its English name. Bark is smooth and silvery; twigs are dark red. Alternate leaves are 12 to 22cm long, oblong and divided about halfway to the midrib into lobes, each with three slender teeth. They are matt green above and grey with hairs in the vein axils below; the petiole is 25 to 50mm long. Acorns ripen in the second year and sit in shallow, 18 to 25mm diameter cups with closely pressed, oval scales. Flowers in May. Native to eastern North America, widely planted in central Europe for ornament, timber and shelter.

Scarlet Oak *Quercus coccinea* Up to 25m

The leaves of this tree turn bright scarlet in autumn. Young twigs are hairy becoming glabrous and yellowish with age. Alternate leaves are 9 to 15cm long, oblong to elliptical with three or four pairs of spreading, toothed lobes; they are bright glossy green above, paler and glabrous beneath but for tufts of hairs in the vein-axils, with 30 to 60mm long petioles. Acorns are solitary, on short stalks and ripen in the second year. The cup is 15 to 20mm across with scales closely pressed together and enclosing half the acorn. Flowers in May. It is grown ornamentally in parks and gardens.

Pin Oak *Quercus palustris* Up to 30m

Beautiful autumn colours distinguish this broad tree. The trunk is straight and the twigs are stiff and rather pendant. The alternate leaves are 10 to 15cm long, oblong and deeply cut with jagged-toothed lobes, with a 20 to 50mm long petiole; they are bright green on both sides and turn red in autumn. The acorns ripen in the second year. The cup is 1 to 15mm in diameter and encloses one third of the acorn. Flowers in May. It is native to eastern North America and is planted for timber, mainly in eastern Europe.

Wych Elm *Ulmus glabra* Up to 40m

A familliar, broad tree with widespreading branches. Young twigs are stout and stiffly hairy. The alternate, rounded-elliptical, long-pointed leaves are 10 to 18cm long with stiff hairs above and soft hairs beneath. Each leaf has 10 to 18 pairs of veins and the asymmetric leaf-base has one side curved to overlap the conceal the leaf-stalk. The purplish-red flower clusters appear before the leaves. Fruit is 15 to 20mm long; the seed centrally placed in a papery wing. Flowers in February and March. It is native to most of Europe except Mediterranean islands.

English Elm *Ulmus procera* Up to 35m

A common tree in Britain, hence its name. The bark is brown and fissured and the twigs are persistantly hairy. The alternate, oval to rounded leaves are 10 to 15cm long with a short-pointed tip. The leaf base is asymmetrical but neither side overlaps the leaf petiole; there are 10 to 12 pairs of veins and upper leaf surface is rough while, on the under surface, there is down either side of the veins. The greenish flowers have red anthers; the fruits are 10 to 17mm long with the seed near the tip of the wing. Flowers February and March. Occurs in Britain and other parts of western and central Europe.

Keaki *Zelkova serrata* Up to 30m

This spreading tree is highly branched from as low as 2m; the main branches are almost vertical. Bark is grey and smooth and the young twigs are covered in hairs becoming glabrous with age. Alternate, oval leaves, 5 to 10cm long, have sharply toothed margins and a pointed tip; they turn rich yellow and red in the autumn. The upper leaf surface is dark green with scattered hairs and the under surface has hairs either side of the 7 to 12 pairs of veins. Rounded fruits are 5mm. Flowers in April. Native to Japan and grown in Europe for ornament.

Black Mulberry *Morus nigra* Up to 12m

This familiar fruit tree has a short trunk and twisted branches. The young twigs are hairy and exude a milky latex when cut. Alternate, heart shaped leaves are toothed or lobed, 6 to 20cm long, rough above but with soft hairs beneath. Male and female flowers are borne on the same tree in catkin-like spikes; males are 2.5cm long, females are 1.3cm long. There are four perianth segments, those of female flowers becoming fleshy in fruit. Red, fleshy fruits are 2 to 2.5cm long. Flowers in May. Native to Asia but it is cultivated in Europe.

71

White Mulberry *Morus alba* Up to 15m

The leaves of this tree are food for silkworms. The bark is grey and ridged and the young twigs are hairy when young. The alternate leaves are rounded to ovate with a heart-shaped base; they are 7 to 16cm long, dark green, smooth and glossy above with the under surface bearing hairs on the veins. The flowers are borne in spikes, 3cm long in the male and 1.5cm long in the female. The fruits are white or pinkish and 1 to 2.5cm long. Flowers in May. Native to eastern Asia but often planted as a roadside tree.

Fig *Ficus carica* Up to 8m

Familiar for its fruit, this spreading tree has pale grey bark. Alternate leaves are thick and leathery, 10 to 20cm long, broad and palmately divided into three to five rounded lobes. Flowers are borne on the inside of a hollow, fleshy and swollen pear-shaped structure which forms the young fig. The fruit ripens in the second year and when fully developed is 5 to 8cm long and brownish or violet-green. Flowers from June to September. Native to south-west Asia and possibly to the Mediterranean where it is widely grown for fruit.

Sweet Bay *Laurus nobilis* Up to 20m

The aromatic foliage of this densely branched evergreen gives it its name. Bark is smooth and grey or dull black. Alternate, narrowly oblong-lanceolate leaves are 5 to 10cm long with wavy margins and dotted with numerous tiny oil glands. The short petiole is dark red. The four-petalled flowers are borne in small clusters, the yellowish males and greenish females on different trees. The ovoid green berries are 1 to 1.5cm long and turn black when fully ripe. Flowers from April to June. Native to dry areas of the Mediterranean and cultivated in much of Europe as a pot-herb or clipped shrub.

London Plane *Platanus × hispanica* Up to 35m

A broad, spreading tree, with twisted, horizontal branches. Thin, grey bark regularly flakes away from the trunk to reveal a mosaic of buff and yellow patches. Alternate leaves up to 25 × 25cm are palmately divided less than halfway to the midrib into five triangular lobes with forward-pointing teeth. Flowers form strings of globose heads, the males in two to six yellowish-green heads, the females usually in two crimson heads. The brown fruiting heads are 2.5cm long. Flowers in June. It is of hybrid origin and is a common European street tree.

73

Similar to London Plane and possibly one of its parents. In outline it is broadly domed with drooping lower branches. Pale brown bark flakes to reveal yellowish patches and the trunk is often burred. Leaves are 20 × 20cm and cut to two-thirds of the way to the midrib into five to seven narrow lobes. The lobes are usually coarsely toothed and can sometimes be entire. Flower heads hang in clusters of three to six. Flowers from April to June. It is native to the Balkans and Crete and is often planted as an ornamental and park tree.

Sassafras *Sassafras albidum* Up to 20m

Best known for the aromatic properties of its roots, bark and leaves which smell of vanilla and oranges. This broadly columnar tree has leaves which are variable in shape but generally ovate in outline and divided into two or three lobes. They are bright green but turn golden-yellow in the autumn. Yellowish flowers are borne in clusters on separate trees. Blue-black berries ripen in the autumn and have green basal swellings and reddish stalks. Flowers in May and June. It is native to eastern North America and is grown in Europe as an ornamental and park tree.

Sweet Gum *Liquidambar styraciflua* Up to 25m

Well known in Europe for its autumn colours, this conical tree has grey, fissured and ridged bark. Sweet gum bleeds from cut twigs and branches. Alternate leaves are 8 to 12cm long, deeply palmately five-lobed, the lobes with toothed margins and pointed tips; the under surface is downy on the veins. The leaves are bright green but turn golden-yellow, orange, purple or scarlet in the autumn. The yellowish flowers are produced in ball-like clusters and the 3cm diameter fruits ripen in autumn. Flowers in May. Native to North America and grown in Europe for ornament.

Witch Hazel *Hamamelis mollis* Up to 8m

Sometimes seen as a small tree but more usually as a large, deciduous shrub with spreading branches. The alternate leaves superficially resemble those of hazel; they are ovate and have toothed margins and a short petiole. The flowers are produced in clusters from the leaf axils and appear well before the leaves; they comprise four long and narrow, yellow petals and four short sepals. The fruit capsule contains two, shiny seeds which are released explosively. Flowers in February and March. It is widely planted as an ornamental tree or shrub and is well known for its medicinal properties.

75

Japanese Witch Hazel *Hamamelis japonica* Up to 4m

Sometimes seen as a small tree but more often occurs as a large, deciduous shrub with sprawling, spreading branches. The alternate leaves superficially resemble those of hazel and witch hazel; they are ovate and have shallowly-toothed margins and a short petiole. The leaves turn from green to golden-yellow in the autumn. The flowers are produced in clusters from the leaf axils; they comprise four long and narrow, yellow petals and four short sepals. Flowers mostly in spring but some cultivars flower in autumn, while the leaves are still present.

Persian Ironwood *Parrotia persica* Up to 12m

A broadly spreading, deciduous tree with a short bole. The smooth bark is greyish-brown and flakes to reveal pinkish to yellow patches beneath. Ovate leaves are 10 to 20cm long with the margins barely toothed and usually slightly wavy; they are dark green and glabrous above but sparsely hairy below. The flowers appear before the leaves and are produced in clusters. The fruit comprises two valves, both of which split into two. Flowers in February and March. It is native to Persia and the Caucasus and is widely planted as an ornamental tree in Europe.

Pittosporum *Pittosporum tenuifolium* Up to 7m

An evergreen tree which is also seen growing as a hedging shrub. Bark is greyish; twigs are slightly hairy. Alternate leaves are 2 to 6cm long, ovate and entire; the margins are crinkly and slightly wavy and the texture is tough and leathery. The upper leaf surface is dark green while the lower surface is paler. Flowers are carried in small clusters; each flower has five dark red petals and oblong sepals. Fruit is a globose capsule which is woody and hairy. Flowers in May. It is native to New Zealand and is grown in Europe as a hedging plant in gardens and parks for its attractive leaves.

Karo *Pittosporum crassifolium* Up to 10m

A small, erect evergreen which is sometimes only a shrub. Alternate leaves are 5 to 8cm long, oblong, blunt and leathery; they are dark green above with dense white hairs beneath. Male and female flowers are produced in separate, flowered clusters, all the stalks arising from the same point. Each flower has five dark red, oblong petals. Fruit is a globose capsule 2 to 2.8cm in diameter, woody and white hairy; it opens by four valves when ripe. Flowers in March. It is native to New Zealand and is grown for ornament and shelter in mild parts of western Europe.

Tulip-tree *Liriodendron tulipifera* Up to 45m

This tall tree has a stout, straight trunk and rather cylindrical profile when young. Bark is greyish-brown or slightly orange and ridged with age. Alternate leaves are 7 to 12cm long and have two, rarely one or three, spreading lobes on each side and a square-notched tip. They are bright green above and slightly bluish and waxy beneath. Flowers, 5cm long, resemble yellow-green tulips and comprise nine petal-like perianth segments. Fruit is 5 to 8cm long, narrow and cone-like. Flowers in May and June. Native to North America but grown in Europe for timber and in parks and gardens for ornament.

Katsura Tree *Cercidiphyllum japonicum* Up to 25m

This tree has a rather conical crown and multiple main branches dividing low down. Bark is grey-brown and fissured; the branches curve upwards. Opposite leaves are 8cm long, rounded and heart-shaped at the base; the margins bear rounded teeth and the leaves are green, becoming reddish in the autumn. Flowers appear before the leaves; males are seen as clusters of red stamens while females are clusters of twisted, red styles. Pod-like fruits are green, becoming brown, and occur in clusters of four to six. Flowers in April. Native to Japan and grown in Europe for ornament.

Evergreen Magnolia *Magnolia grandiflora* Up to 30m

This large tree has spreading branches and a conical crown. Smooth bark is dull grey and the young twigs have reddish down. Alternate leaves are 8 to 16cm long, thick, leathery and entire; the edges are sometimes wavy, the upper surface is shiny and the under surface is covered with rusty hairs. The fragrant flowers are up to 25cm across and comprise six petal-like segments; they are initially conical but open flat. Single-seeded fruits form cone-like structures 5 to 6cm long. Flowers from July to November. Native to North America and grown in Europe for ornament.

Common Pear *Pyrus communis* Up to 20m

A narrow, suckering tree. Young twigs are slightly hairy but become glabrous and reddish with age. Alternate leaves are 5 to 8cm long, pointed and oval-elliptical; they have finely toothed margins, are hairy when unfurling, but become glabrous. The flowers appear in clusters with the leaves; they comprise five white petals, 12 to 14mm long and reddish-purple anthers. The fruits range from 4 to 12cm in length, are pear-shaped to globose and yellowish-brown. Flowers in April. Its origins are in Asia but it is widely cultivated and naturalised in Europe.

Sage-leaved Pear *Pyrus salvifolia* Up to 10m

A small, spreading tree. Young twigs are grey and hairy but become dark and more glabrous with age. The branches are usually spiny. Leaves are 4 to 7cm long, elliptical and entire; the upper surface is smooth while the under surface has woolly hairs. Clusters of flowers appear with the leaves and comprise five white petals. The fruit is 6 to 8cm long, pear-shaped and furry or woolly, especially when young. Flowers in April. It is naturalised sparingly throughout Europe and is often cultivated.

Pyrus eleagrifolia Up to 10m

A slender tree, often no more than a shrub. Twigs are hairy; branches usually spiny. Alternate leaves are 3.5 to 8cm long, more-or-less lanceolate and toothed at the tip or entire; they have a short petiole and are covered with dense grey-white wool even when mature. The flowers appear with the leaves, in more-or-less stalk-less clusters. There are five, white petals, each 10mm long. Fruit is about 1.3cm long and is pear-shaped or globular, green when ripe with a thick stalk. Flowers in April. Native to the Balkans, Turkey and Russia.

Plymouth Pear *Pyrus cordata* Up to 8m

Often only a shrub, this small tree has spreading branches and almost glabrous twigs. Alternate leaves are 2.5 to 5.5cm long, oval, with a toothed margin; the petiole is 2.5cm long and the leaves are hairy only when young. Flowers appear in slender clusters with the leaves. There are five, white petals, each 6 to 8mm long and sepals that drop. Fruit is pearshaped, carried on a slender stalk and lacks persistant sepals. Flowers in April. It is native to France, the Iberian Peninsula and Britain, where it is extremely rare and only found growing in south Devon and Cornwall.

Cultivated Apple *Malus domestica* Up to 15m

A well-known orchard tree producing the familiar edible fruits. Bark is brown and the twigs are hairy. Alternate leaves are oval or elliptical, pointed, slightly toothed and 4 to 13cm long; they are sparsely hairy above and woolly below. The five-petalled flowers are pink or occasionally white, 3 to 4cm across and appear in clusters with the leaves. Both the flower stalks and the outer surface of the persistant sepals are densely hairy. Fruit is more than 5cm long and varies from green to red or brown. Flowers in May and June. Of hybrid origin, divided into thousands of cultivars and grown throughout Europe.

Crab Apple *Malus sylvestris* 2 to 10m

This familiar, spreading tree has a dense crown and large, twisted branches. Bark is brown and cracks into scales. Alternate, toothed leaves are 3 to 11cm long and oval; they are glabrous on both surfaces when mature. The five-petalled flowers are 3 to 4cm across and appear with the leaves. The persistant sepals have thick hair on the inner surface. Fruit is 2.5 to 3cm long and yellowish-green flushed with red; it is hard and sour. Flowers in May and June. It is native to chalky hills in much of Europe and anciently domesticated and widely naturalised. It is a parent of the hybrid orchard apple.

Japanese Crab Apple *Malus × floribunda* 6 to 9m

A stunning tree which produces masses of blossom in spring. Bark is greyish-brown; twigs are reddish when young and densely hairy. Alternate leaves are 4 to 8cm long, oblong to oval, pointed, toothed or sometimes even lobed. The undersides are downy at first. Clusters of flowers appear with or just after the leaves. Buds are deep pink, the flowers have five petals. The deciduous petals are hairy on the inner surface. Fruit is up to 2.5cm long, ripening yellow. Flowers in April and May. It is a garden hybrid from Japan and is widely grown for ornament in Europe.

Siberian Crab Apple *Malus baccata* Up to 15m

A short, broadly spreading tree producing an abundance of flowers in spring. Bark is greyish-brown and flaky. Alternate leaves are ovate, 6 to 8cm long, finely toothed and with a pointed tip; both surfaces are glabrous, the upper being darker green than the under surface. Clusters of flowers appear with the leaves. Individual flowers are 4cm across and comprise five white petals, tinged pink when opening. The small, rounded fruits are 1cm across and initially green but becoming bright red when ripe. Native to eastern Asia and is sometimes grown for ornament in Europe.

Hawthorn-leaved Crab Apple *Malus florentina* Up to 4m

This small tree lacks spines or thorns. Alternate leaves are 3 to 6cm long, broadly oval in outline with the base heart-shaped or cut straight across; the margins are toothed with several sharp, irregular lobes on each side. Upper leaf surface is dark green; the lower has dense white hairs. Petiole is 0.5 to 2cm long. The flower is 1 to 2cm long and has five white petals and deciduous sepals. Fruit is about 1cm long, ellipsoid to pear-shaped and red when ripe with gritty flesh. Flowers in April and May. Native from Italy to northern Greece and sometimes grown for ornament.

Hupeh Crab Apple *Malus hupehensis* Up to 12m

This broadly spreading tree produces large quantities of blossom in spring. Bark is deep brown and flaky. Alternate leaves are ovate, 8 to 10cm long, finely toothed and with a pointed tip; they are glabrous and dark green above. Clusters of flowers appear with the leaves. Individual flowers are cup-shaped, 5cm in diameter when open and comprise five, white petals which overlap slightly; in bud, the flowers are pink. The rounded, red fruit is 1cm across and persistant. Flowers in April and May. It is native to China and is sometimes grown for ornament in Europe.

John Downie Crab Apple *Malus 'John Downie'* Up to 10m

One of the best known and most popular of a range of cultivated hybrids, the result of crossing between various species. Alternate leaves are ovate, 10cm long, finely toothed and with a pointed tip; they are glabrous and dark green. Clusters of flowers appear with the leaves and are 5cm in diameter with five petals. The buds are pink and the petals are white. The fruits are rather ovoid, 3 to 4cm long and yellowish-orange, becoming reddish when ripe. Flowers in April and May. It is widely grown as an ornamental tree both for its flowers and its fruits.

Malus × zumi Up to 10m

This hybrid crab apple is best known for its small fruits, the main reason why it is grown. Alternate leaves are ovate, 6 to 10cm long with a pointed tip and margins bearing rounded teeth; they are glabrous and dark green. Clusters of flowers appear with the leaves and are 20 to 30cm in diameter with five petals. The buds are pinkish and the petals are white. The fruits are rounded, 5 to 10mm across and becoming reddish when ripe; they resemble miniature cherries. Flowers in April and May. It is grown as an ornamental tree in some parts of Europe.

Quince *Cydonia oblonga* Up to 7.5m

The trunk of this tree or shrub is short and slender with grey-brown bark. Young shoots are spiny and woolly, becoming glabrous later. Alternate, oval leaves are 5 to 10cm long, entire and grey and woolly below. The pink or white flowers are solitary and are carried on short, hairy stalks; they are cup-shaped with five broad, blunt or notched petals. Pear-shaped, yellow fruits are 2.5 to 3.5cm long in wild plants but up to 12cm in cultivated forms. Flowers in May. It is native to Asia but is common in the Mediterranean countries. It is cultivated in much of Europe and has become naturalised.

Loquat *Eriobotrya japonica* Up to 10m

A small tree or shrub with coarse, evergreen foliage. The twigs and undersides of the leaves are covered with velvety, rusty hairs. Alternate leaves are 10 to 25cm long, elliptical to oblong with toothed margins; the upperside is dark, glossy green. Fragrant flowers, 1cm long, are borne in pyramidal clusters at the tips of shoots. They comprise five yellowish-white petals that may be almost hidden by reddish hairs. Fruits are 3 to 6cm long and resemble apricots. Flowers from November to April. It is native to China and is widely cultivated in southern Europe for fruit and ornament.

Medlar *Mespilus germanica* Up to 6m

This tree or spreading shrub has a dense, tangled crown. Bark is grey-brown and cracked and the young twigs have dense white hairs; older twigs are black and glabrous. Alternate leaves are 5 to 15cm long, yellowish, crinkled and lance-shaped; entire or minutely toothed. Flowers are 3 to 6cm across with broad white petals. Brown fruits are 2 to 3cm long, globose, with a depression surrounded by persistent sepals; the fruits persist on the tree. Flowers in May and June. It is native to south-eastern Europe but is widely cultivated elsewhere.

Hawthorn *Crategus monogyna* Up to 18m

Frequently cut back to form hedges, this thorny tree is dense with pale grey-brown bark. Branches bear numerous twigs up to 15mm long. Alternate, shiny leaves are 1.5 to 4.5cm long, one and a half times as long as broad and divided into three to seven lobes; the lobes are entire or toothed near the tip. The five-petalled flowers are 8 to 15mm across, white to pale pink, each with a single style. Red fruits are 7 to 14mm long, globose to ovoid and contain a single seed. Flowers in May and June. Native throughout Europe.

Oriental Hawthorn *Crategus laciniata* Up to 10m

This small tree is often just a shrub. The grey-brown bark is reddish between the cracks. Twigs have white hairs when young. Alternate leaves are 1.5 to 4cm long, oval, and divided into three to seven narrow, toothed lobes. They are hairy, leathery and dull green above. Flowers are 1.5 to 2cm across and are produced in clusters on white-haired stalks. There are five white petals, four to five styles and hooked-tip sepals. The 15 to 20mm long fruits ripen yellowish-orange and contain three to five seeds. Flowers in June. Native to south-eastern Europe, Sicily and Spain.

Azarole *Crategus azarolus* Up to 8m

The young twigs of this small tree or shrub are covered with dense, short hairs but become glabrous with 1cm spines. Alternate leaves are hairy, 3 to 5cm long, oval and deeply divided into three to five narrow lobes; the leaf base often continues down the petiole. The 1.2 to 1.8cm diameter, white flowers are carried in clusters of 3 to 18, each comprising five petals. The 20 to 25mm long, orange-red fruits resemble small apples; each containing one to three seeds. Fowers in March and April. Native to Crete and western Asia but is anciently cultivated in southern Europe.

Cockspur Thorn *Crategus crus-galli* Up to 10m

This rather small tree has a short trunk and a low, spreading crown. Bark is smooth and greyish-brown; the twigs are armed with 7 to 10cm thorns. Alternate leaves are 5 to 8cm long, with toothed margins and glabrous on both surfaces; they turn bright orange in autumn. The 1.5cm diameter flowers are carried on glabrous stalks in loose clusters; there are five white petals and two styles. Red fruits are 10 to 12mm long, globose and persist through the winter; each contains two seeds. Flowers in May. Native to North America and widely planted in Europe for ornament.

Hybrid Cockspur Thorn *Crategus × lavallei* Up 21m

A sturdy, leafy tree with few spines and downy twigs. The alternate leaves are oval or widest above the middle, irregularly toothed, dark green, glossy above and downy beneath. The white, 2cm diameter flowers have very woolly stalks and sepals, five petals and one to three styles. The fruits are 16 to 18mm long, orange to red speckled with brown, globose to pear-shaped and persist through the winter. Flowers in June. It probably has cockspur thorn as one of its parents and was first cultivated in 1880. It is widely planted for ornament.

Snowy Mespil *Amelanchier ovalis* Up to 5m

Sometimes a small tree but usually a shrub. The young twigs are woolly and spineless. Alternate leaves are oval, 2.5 to 5cm long with coarsely toothed margins; the under surface is woolly in young leaves. Flowers appear with the leaves in clusters of three to eight; they comprise five white petals. The juicy fruits are blackish, sometimes with a grape-like bloom, and are crowned with persistent sepals. Flowers in April and May. It grows in woodland, mountains and rocky areas. It is native to limestone regions of southern and central Europe and is sometimes grown for ornament.

Rowan *Sorbus aucuparia* 5 to 20m

A bushy tree with a rounded, open crown and spreading branches. Alternate leaves are pinnately divided into five to ten pairs of oblong leaflets, each 3 to 6cm long; the leaflet blades are toothed in the upper part, asymmetric at the base with grey hairs below. The flowers are 8 to 10mm across with five white petals and three to four styles. The globose or oval fruits are 6 to 9mm long and scarlet. Flowers in May. It is native to most of Europe, growing on wooded habitats in all but the most waterlogged situations. It is also planted in towns and is popular as a street tree.

Hupeh Rowan *Sorbus hupehensis* Up to 14m

This bushy tree with a rounded crown is similar in outline to Rowan but differs in its leaves and fruits. Slightly drooping leaves are pinnately divided into five to six pairs of oblong, bluish-green leaflets, each 3.7 to 7.5cm long and sharply toothed towards their tips. The leaf-axis is reddish and grooved and the leaves turn red in the autumn. Globose fruits are about 6mm long, white or pale pink and persist on the twigs into winter. Flowers in May. Native to western China and is planted in Europe for ornament in parks and gardens.

Wild Service-tree *Sorbus torminalis* Up to 25m

A domed tree or a large, spreading shrub. Bark is scaly and the twigs are shiny brown. Alternate leaves are 5 to 10cm long, oval with three to five pairs of toothed, pointed lobes, the lowest pair deeper and more wide-spreading than the others; they are dark green above and hairy beneath only when young. Flowers, 10 to 15mm diameter, have five white petals, two styles and are borne on woolly stalks in branched clusters. The fleshy brown fruits are 12 to 18mm long and are dotted with lenticels. Flowers in May and June. Native but scattered throughout Europe.

Whitebeam *Sorbus aria* Up to 25m

A rather pallid tree, especially in spring when the white undersides of the leaves are most noticeable. Alternate leaves are 5 to 12cm long, oval with irregular teeth curving towards the rounded tip; they are bright green above and white felted beneath with 10 to 14 pairs of veins. The 10 to 15mm diameter flowers have five white petals and are borne in branched clusters. Ovoid fruits are 8 to 15mm long, scarlet, with many small lenticels. Flowers in May and June. Native to most of Europe, occuring mainly on limestone. Ornamental varieties are grown in parks and are popular as street trees.

Rock Whitebeam *Sorbus rupicola* Up to 15m

A small tree or sometimes just a hedgerow shrub. Alternate leaves are 8 to 14.5cm long, oval, widest above the middle and with seven to nine pairs of veins; the margins are not lobed but bear forward-pointed teeth. The upper leaf surface is dark green and the under surface is white-woolly. The white flowers have five petals and are borne in branched clusters. Fruits are 12 to 15mm long, red and globose, with numerous lenticels. Flowers in May and June. It is native to Britain and Scandinavia and is occasionally grown for ornament.

Swedish Whitebeam *Sorbus intermedia* Up to 15m

This rounded tree has a short trunk and a domed crown. Young twigs are densely hairy but glabrous later. Alternate leaves are 6 to 12cm long with elliptical lobes, those near the base cut one third of the way to the midrib and those towards the tip progressively shallower, eventually reduced to coarse teeth. Flowers are 12 to 20mm across, white with five petals and carried in flattened clusters. The ovoid fruits are 12 to 15mm long, scarlet with few lenticels. Flowers in May. It is native to Scandinavia but, being pollution-tolerant, is planted as a street tree elsewhere.

Devonshire Whitebeam *Sorbus devoniensis* Up to 10m

A rounded tree with a relatively short trunk and a dense, domed crown. Alternate leaves are 7 to 10cm long and ovate, with shallow lobes usually cut less than one quarter of the way to the midrib; those towards the tip become progressively shallower. Leaves are smooth and dark green above but paler and slightly downy beneath. Flowers are 12 to 18mm across, white with five petals. Ovoid fruits are 10 to 15mm long, orange-brown with numerous lenticels. Flowers in May and June. It is native to woodlands in parts of the West Country and southern Ireland.

Blackthorn *Prunus spinosa* Up to 6m

As its name suggests, this small tree or shrub has dense, wide-spreading, thorny branches. Trunk produces numerous suckers and the twigs are downy when young but glabrous and smooth with age. Alternate, toothed leaves are 2 to 4.5cm long and oval; they are dull and glabrous above but hairy on the veins beneath. Flowers are solitary, appearing well before the leaves. They comprise five white petals 5 to 8mm long. Astringent fruit is 1 to 1.5cm long, bluish-black with a greyish bloom. Flowers in March and April. Native throughout Europe, except the far north.

Almond *Prunus dulcis* Up to 8m

Profuse blossom adorns this open-crowned tree or shrub. Wild trees have spiny branches, unarmed in cultivated trees. Alternate leaves are 4 to 13cm long, finely toothed and folded lengthways. Flowers, mostly paired, appear before the leaves. They form a short, bell-shaped tube comprising five petals, 15 to 25mm long; these are usually pale pink but fade white with age. Oblong-oval fruit is grey-green and 3.5 to 6cm long; its large pitted stone is the familiar almond. Flowers in March and April. Probably native to Asia but has long been cultivated in southern Europe.

Japanese Cherry *Prunus serrulata* Up to 15m

A beautiful tree in spring when it is covered in blossom. Bark is reddish or purple-brown with horizontal bands of lenticels. The twigs are glabrous. Alternate leaves are oval, 8 to 20 cm long, dark shiny green above and bluish below; the margins bear pointed teeth. Flowers appear before the leaves in clusters of two to four; they are white or pink, often double and the petals are 1.5 to 4cm long with a notched tip. Dark red fruits are rarely produced. Flowers in May. Probably native to China, developed in Japan, and is now popular in Europe.

Sargent's Cherry *Prunus sargentii* Up to 25m

Similar to Japanese Cherry and, in the same way, often not attaining its full height in cultivation. Purplish-brown bark has horizontal lenticels. Alternate leaves are 9 to 15cm long, almost oblong and dark, shiny green above but bluish-green below; the margins have, sharp, spreading teeth. Rose-pink petals are 15 to 20cm long, without a notched tip. Fruits are 7 to 11mm long, ovoid and blackish-crimson and not often produced in cultivation. Flowers in April. It is native to Japan and is widely grown in Europe as an ornamental tree in streets and parks.

Tibetan Cherry *Prunus serrula* Up to 20m

One of the most attractive barks of all cherries distinguishes this tree. It is purplish-black but peeling away in bands to leave a highly polished reddish mahogany colour beneath. Leaves are 6 to 10cm long, lanceolate and slightly toothed with a long, pointed tip; the petioles are only 6 to 7mm long. White flowers appear with the leaves; the petals are 8 to 10mm long and are carried on 4cm long stalks. Fruits are 4 to 12mm long and ripen bright red. Flowers in April and May. Native to western China and is widespread as a park and garden tree.

95

Wild Cherry *Prunus avium* Up to 30m

A large cherry tree with a well-developed trunk and shiny, red-brown bark peeling in horizontal bands. Alternate leaves are oval, 8 to 15cm long and abruptly pointed with blunt, forward-pointing teeth. Veins on the underside have tufts of hairs in the angles. The 2 to 3cm diameter flowers appear just before the leaves in clusters of two to six. The five white petals are 1 to 1.5cm long. Fruits, 9 to 12mm long, are usually dark red but sometimes yellowish or even black. Flowers in April and May. Native to most of Europe and widely cultivated for its fruit.

Bird Cherry *Prunus padus* Up to 17m

The smooth, grey-brown bark of this tree has an unpleasant smell. Alternate, oblong to elliptical leaves are 6 to 10cm long, slightly leathery, dark green above, paler or bluish below with a tapering point and sharp, fine-toothed margins. The flowers appear after the leaves in elongated spikes of 7 to 15cm containing 15 to 35 white, almond-scented flowers with five petals, 6 to 9mm long. Fruits are 6 to 8mm long and shiny black. Flowers in May. Native to most of Europe, growing in woods and hedgerows, and is sometimes planted for ornament.

Spring Cherry *Prunus subhirtella* Up to 20m

This dense, bushy-crowned tree, seldom attains its full height in cultivation. Twigs are slender, crimson and downy. Alternate leaves are 6cm long, oval, with a long-pointed tip and irregular teeth; they have a crimson petiole and downy veins on the underside of the leaf. Flowers appear before the leaves in clusters of two to five; the petals are 8 to 12mm long, pink and notched. Fruit is 7 to 9mm long, ripening purplish-black. Flowers in March and April but some specimens, distinguished as Autumn Cherry, flower from October to April. Native to Japan and widely grown for ornament.

Cherry Laurel *Prunus laurocerasus* up to 8m

The leaves of this small, spreading evergreen, smell of almonds when crushed. The alternate, oblong to lanceolate leaves are 10 to 20cm long, leathery, dark and glossy green above and yellowish-green below; the margins are rolled-under, entire or minutely toothed and the petioles are green. The fragrant flowers are carried in upright spikes, equal in length to the leaves. Five, white petals are about 4mm long. The globose red fruits are 2cm long and ripen shiny black. Flowers in April. It is native to the Balkans and is grown for ornament in much of Europe.

Cherry Plum *Prunus cerasifera* Up to 8m

Often mistaken for Blackthorn, this rounded tree or shrub suckers readily. Young twigs are smooth and green and the branches are slender and often spiny. The alternate, oval leaves are 4 to 7cm long and taper at both ends; they have small, rounded teeth and are smooth and glossy above but downy on the veins beneath. Solitary flowers appear before the leaves. The five petals are 8 to 10mm long and white to pale pink. The smooth, globose fruit is 3.5cm long and yellow or red. Flowers in March. Native to the Balkans and is widely planted and naturalised elsewhere.

Blackwood *Acacia melanoxylon* Up to 15m

This robust evergreen has a straight, rough-barked trunk. Alternate, dark green leaves are 6 to 13cm long, lanceolate but blunt and slightly curved; they have three to five veins. Pinnately divided leaves occasionally appear on young trees. Minute flowers are massed in creamy-white, spherical heads, 10mm across; these are borne in axillary clusters. Red-brown pods are 7 to 12cm long, 8 to 10mm wide, flattened and twisted; the seeds have scarlet stalks. Flowers from July to October. It is native to south-eastern Australia but planted for timber and naturalised in south-western Europe.

Swamp Wattle *Acacia retinoides* Up to 10m

This small tree or shrub has characteristically upcurving branches. The leaves are 6 to 14cm long, less than 2cm wide, lanceolate but blunt and slightly curved. The flowers are very small but are massed in pale yellow, spherical heads, 4 to 6mm across; these are borne in axillary clusters. The reddish-brown pods are constricted slightly between the seeds; the seed stalks are scarlet. Flowers in June and July. It is native to southern Australia and is widely planted for ornament in southern Europe where it occasionally becomes naturalised.

Sydney Golden Wattle *Acacia longifolia* Up to 10m

A slender evergreen with a bushy, spreading crown. Grey bark is smooth; twigs are stiff and glabrous. Alternate leaves are green, 7 to 15cm long, narrowly oblong with prominent, parallel veins. Flowers are bright yellow and strong-smelling; they are grouped in erect, cylindrical spikes up to 5cm long. Narrow, cylindrical pod is 7 to 15cm long, may be straight or twisted and curled and is sometimes constricted between the white-stalked seeds. Flowers in April and May. It is native to coastal New South Wales in Australia and is grown in south-western Europe as a dune-stabiliser and ornament.

False Acacia *Robinia pseudacacia* Up to 25m

The short trunks of this crowned tree are often multiple and the bark is spirally-ridged. Alternate leaves are 15 to 20cm long, pinnate with three to ten pairs of oval-elliptical yellowish-green leaflets; the petiole has two woody, spiny stipules at the base and each leaflet has a tiny stipule at the petiole base. White, fragrant, pea-like flowers form dense, hanging clusters 10 to 20cm long. The smooth, 5 to 10cm long pods persist on the tree. Flowers in June. Native to North America and is widely planted in southern Europe as a street street, occasionally becoming naturalised.

Clammy Locust *Robinia viscosa* Up to 12m

An open-crowned deciduous tree. Bark is brown and the young twigs are stickily hairy and armoured with thorns. Alternate leaves are 15 to 25cm long, pinnate with three to ten pairs of oval to elliptical yellowish-green leaflets; the petiole is sticky and hairy at the base. Pea-like flowers are pink, fragrant, and carried in dense, hanging clusters up to 13cm long. The pods are 5 to 10cm long, sticky and hairy; they are brown and contain reddish-brown seeds. Flowers in June. Native to North America and is planted as an ornamental tree in central and southern Europe.

Pagoda-tree *Sophora japonica* Up to 25m

An open-crowned tree with twisted branches. Bark is furrowed; twigs are bluish-green and hairy when young. Alternate leaves are 15 to 25cm long, pinnate with three to eight pairs of oval, pointed leaflets; these are dark shiny green above and bluish-hairy beneath. Pea-like flowers are 10 to 15mm long, white or pale pink, and carried in large clusters 15 to 25cm across at the twig tips. The pod is 5 to 8cm long and greenish. Flowers in August and September. Native to eastern Asia and is planted for ornament in Europe where it is sometimes naturalised.

Carob *Ceratonia siliqua* Up to 10m

A low evergreen tree with a domed crown. Alternate leaves are pinnate with two to five pairs of leathery leaflets. Each leaflet is 3 to 5cm long, oval and notched at the tip; the margins are often wavy and they are dark shiny green above and pale beneath. Tiny flowers are grouped in short, green, unisexual spikes; they lack petals and the five sepals soon fall leaving only a central disc bearing either stamens or a style. Ripe pods are 10 to 20cm long, violet-brown with seeds embedded in a white pulp. Flowers from August to October. Native to the Mediterranean.

Honey Locust *Gleditsia triacanthos* Up to 45m

A tall tree, armoured with large spines. Bark is brown with vertical cracks. Alternate leaves are either pinnate with 7 to 18 pairs of leaflets each 20 to 30mm long, or twice-pinnate, each pinna with 8 to 14 pairs of leaflets only 8 to 20mm long; there is no terminal leaflet, the leaf-axis ending in a spine. Flowers, 3mm long, comprise three to five greenish-white, oval petals and form dense axillary clusters. Pods are 30 to 45cm long, flattened and curved. Flowers in June. Native to North America and cultivated in southern and central Europe.

Caspian Locust *Gleditsia capsica* Up to 12m

A short, broadly spreading deciduous tree with large spines; those on the trunk are long and branched and are usually in large groups. The bark is brown and sometimes cracked vertically. Alternate, fern-like leaves are usually pinnate, each pinna with 8 to 14 pairs of leaflets; the upper surface is glossy. The flowers have three to five greenish-white petals and form axillary clusters. Flowers in May and June. It is native to western Asia and is grown for ornament in some parts of Europe.

Laburnum *Laburnum anagyroides* Up to 7m

A small and slender tree with ascending or arching branches. Both twigs and leaves are grey-green with silky, close-pressed hairs. Alternate leaves are tri-foliate, the elliptical leaflets each 3 to 8cm long. Pea-like flowers are 3cm long, yellow and fragrant, forming pendulous clusters 10 to 30cm long. The pods are 4 to 6cm long, and smooth and dark brown when ripe. They persist on the tree after splitting, exposing the paler inner surfaces and poisonous black seeds. Flowers in May and June. Native to southern and central Europe and widely planted elsewhere.

Judas-tree *Cercis siliquastrum* Up to 10m

A slender, spreading tree, often with several trunks. Alternate leaves are 7 to 12cm long, almost circular, heart-shaped at the base, bluish-green when young, turning dark or yellowish-green above. The pink flowers are 15 to 20mm long and comprise five, unequal petals, the upper erect and the side pair overlapping the fused, boat-shaped lower pair; they appear with or before the leaves. Pods are 6 to 10cm long and ripen purplish-brown. Flowers in May. Native to the Mediterranean and is often grown elsewhere for ornament.

Orange *Citrus sinensis* Up to 10m

The familiar fruit orange grows on this rounded, often bushy, tree. Twigs are angled, sometimes with thin, blunt spines. Alternate leaves are 7.5 to 10cm long, oval to elliptical, dark glossy green above, firm, leathery and dotted with shiny oil glands. The petiole is short with a prominent wing. White, fragrant flowers are solitary or in loose clusters in the leaf-axils, and appear with the fruit. The fruit is about 7.5cm across and thick-skinned. Flowers mainly in May, but in other months depending on the variety. It is native to eastern Asia but is grown all around the Mediterranean.

Lemon *Citrus limon* Up to 10m

Similar in overall appearance to orange tree and produces the familiar fruit, lemon. Leathery leaves are about 10cm long with minutely toothed margins; there is usually a thick, stiff spine at the base of the short petiole which lacks a wing. Small white flowers are flushed purple or reddish on the outside. Fruit is oval, 7 to 12cm long with a protruding apex, yellow when ripe and has juicy flesh that remains sour. Flowers more-or-less throughout the year. Its origins are obscure but it is widely cultivated throughout the Mediterranean.

Stag's-horn Sumach *Rhus typhina* Up to 10m

This small tree or shrub often suckers or has several trunks. Branches are curved, young twigs are velvety-hairy. Alternate leaves are pinnately divided into 11 to 29 drooping leaflets, each 5 to 12cm long, narrowly oval, pointed, toothed and softly hairy; they turn bright red and orange in autumn. Flowers have five petals; males are greenish, females are red. They are carried in 10 to 20cm long conical heads. Nut-like fruits, 4mm, are carried in dense, dull crimson heads up to 20cm long. Flowers from May to July. Native to North America and grown in Europe for ornament.

Mastic-tree *Pistacia lentiscus* Up to 8m

The leaves and fruit of this evergreen are highly aromatic. Glabrous twigs are warty. Alternate leaves are pinnately divided into three to six pairs of leaflets; the narrowly winged leaf-axis ends in a short spine and the petiole is downy. Leaflets are dark green, 1 to 5cm long, narrowly oval and tipped with a short spine. Flowers are carried in dense, spiky axillary heads 2 to 5cm long; they are yellow-tinged to purplish and lack petals. Fruits, 4mm long, are globose with a spike-like tip; bright red when young, ripening black. Flowers in April. Native to the Mediterranean and Portugal.

105

Turpentine-tree *Pistacia terebinthus* Up to 10m

This small tree or shrub has grey bark and stickily resinous twigs. Leaves are resin-scented. Alternate leaves are pinnately divided into three to nine leaflets and the leaf-axis is cylindrical, ending in a leaflet. Leaflets are leathery, dark and shiny, and each 2 to 8cm long, oval-oblong and spine-tipped. Flowers are carried in loose, long-branched clusters; they appear before the leaves, are brownish-purple and lack petals. Fruits are 5 to 7mm long, pear-shaped; coral red when young, ripening brown. Flowers in March and April. Native to the Mediterranean and Portugal.

Pistachio *Pistachio vera* Up to 6m

Famous for its edible seeds, this tree or shrub has rough, ridged bark. Alternate leaves undivided or pinnate with three to five leaflets and a narrowly winged axis. Leaflets are 4 to 9cm long, broadly oval and grey-green; initially downy but soon glabrous. Flowers are carried in loose, long-branched clusters; they appear before the leaves, are brownish and lack petals. Hard-shelled fruits are 2 to 2.5cm long, ovoid, tipped with a slender point and pale reddish-brown when ripe; they contain a single seed. Flowers in April. Native to western Asia. Widely grown in the Mediterranean.

Sycamore *Acer pseudoplatanus* Up to 35m

A fast-growing, invasive tree with a wide-spreading crown that is often broader than it is high. Twigs are grey-green. Opposite leaves are 10 to 15cm long, with five coarsely toothed lobes. The flowers are greenish-yellow and appear with the leaves, hanging in separate male and female clusters 6 to 12cm long. Fruits are borne in pairs 3.5 to 5cm long, the grey-brown wings making an angle of 90 degrees. Flowers in April and May. It is native to central and southern Europe but is widely planted and often naturalised elsewhere in the region. It tolerates salt spray and is often planted near the sea.

Silver Maple *Acer saccharinum* Up to 35m

An elegant tree with a tall, spreading crown. Trunk has smooth, grey-brown bark becoming shaggy with age and the twigs are brown or purplish. Opposite leaves are 9 to 16cm long, with five deeply and irregularly toothed lobes; they are green above with silver hairs beneath. Red or greenish flowers appear before the leaves, the short stalked males and long stalked females in separate clusters of four to five; both sexes lack petals. Fruits are 5cm long and paired, the green, strongly veined wings diverging at a narrow angle. Flowers in March. Native to North America but commonly planted in Europe.

107

Norway Maple *Acer platanoides* Up to 30m

A sycamore-like tree, colourful both in spring and autumn. Trunk is short with greyish, smooth or fissured bark. Twigs are dull green tinged with red. The opposite leaves are 10 to 15cm long, with five to seven slender-toothed lobes. The yellowish-green flowers appear before the leaves in erect clusters, males and females separate; there are five sepals and five petals. Yellowish fruits are 3 to 5cm long and paired, the wings forming a wide angle or horizontal. Flowers in April. Native to much of Europe but not Britain. Widely planted as a street or park tree.

Field Maple *Acer campestre* Up to 25m

A small tree or a large hedgerow shrub. Trunk is twisted; twigs are brown and finely hairy. Opposite leaves are 4 to 12cm long, usually three-lobed, the outer lobe often further lobed, all with rounded teeth towards the tip. Young leaves are pinkish, becoming dark green when mature and turning yellowish or reddish in autumn. The yellowish-green flowers have five sepals and five petals; they appear with the leaves, both sexes together in erect clusters. Fruits are 2 to 4cm long, paired, the green- or red-winged wings spreading horizontally. Flowers in April and May. Native to northern Europe.

108

Montpelier Maple *Acer monspessulanum* Up to 12m

A small tree or shrub with a domed crown. Bark is dark and cracked; twigs are thin and brown. Opposite leaves are up to 8cm long, with three oval, entire lobes; the lateral lobes form a wide angle with the middle lobes. Mature leaves are leathery, dark green above, greyish-blue beneath. Yellowish-green flowers are borne on long stalks and appear after the leaves. Males and females are in separate clusters, both lack petals and are erect then drooping. Fruits are 1 to 2cm long, paired, with parallel wings that are greenish then crimson-tinged. Flowers in June and is scattered throughout southern Europe.

Caucasian Maple *Acer cappadocium* Up to 20m

A smallish, broadly spreading tree which is stunning in autumn. Trunk is relatively short; bark is smooth and greyish. Opposite leaves are up to 10cm long with five to seven oval, entire lobes which are heart-shaped; these are bright green above, the under surface having hairs in the vein axils. In autumn, the leaves turn bright yellow before dropping. Yellowish flowers are carried in upright clusters and appear with the leaves. Fruits are 3 to 4cm long, paired, with wide-spreading wings. Flowers in June. Native to western Asia but is widely planted for ornament in parks and gardens.

Paper-bark Maple *Acer griseum* Up to 15m

The bark of this columnar tree is cinnamon-coloured and peels off in thin papery layers exposing the reddish younger bark. Opposite leaves are 10cm long and have three, toothed leaflets; the upper surface is dark green while the under surface is bluish-white and coated with soft hairs. The leaves turn red in the autumn. Small, yellowish flowers are borne in drooping clusters; they appear with the leaves. Fruits are 3cm long and paired, with narrowly-spreading wings. Flowers in June. Native to China and is widely planted for ornament.

Box-elder *Acer negundo* up to 20m

This fast-growing tree has an irregularly domed crown. Short trunk often has swellings; the bark is grey, becoming darker and cracked with age. Opposite leaves are pinnate, 10 to 15cm long, with five to seven oval, pointed and toothed leaflets. Red male and greenish female flowers apear before the leaves on different trees; both sexes lack petals. Fruits are 2cm long and paired, with wings forming a narrow angle. Flowers in March. Native to eastern North America but widely planted in Europe for ornament or street tree, cultivars with variegated leaves being favoured.

Moosewood *Acer pennsylvanicum* Up to 8m

This columnar tree is a favourite food of the moose in its native North America. Bark is greenish and vertically striped with white. Opposite leaves are 15cm long, roughly heart-shaped but divided into three, long-pointed lobes. They are dark green in summer but turn bright yellow in the autumn. The flowers are small, yellowish-green and are borne in long, drooping chains; they appear after the leaves, males and females separately. Fruits are 2.5cm long, the wings forming a narrow angle. Flowers in May. Grown as an ornamental tree, for its bark and leaf colour.

Nikko Maple *Acer nikoense* Up to 20m

Colourful autumn foliage distinguishes this spreading tree. Bark is grey and smooth. Opposite leaves have three, oval and usually untoothed leaflets, the central leaflet 10cm in length; they are smooth above but downy-hairy beneath. In summer, the leaves are dark green but turn red in autumn before falling. Flowers are small, yellow and borne in clusters of three; they appear with the leaves. Fruits are 4 to 5cm long and have broad, widely spreading, green wings. Flowers in May. Native to Japan and is grown for ornament, also being known as *Acer maximowiczianum*.

111

Smooth Japanese Maple *Acer palmatum* Up to 15m

This small, rounded tree, often has a twisted trunk. Young twigs are reddish above and green below. Opposite leaves are 6 to 9cm long and divided into five to seven oval or lanceolate lobes, cut more than halfway to the base; the margins are sharply toothed. Reddish flowers are borne in clusters of 12 to 15; each flower is 6 to 9mm across and carried on a long stalk. Fruits are 3cm long and have broad, widely spreading wings. Flowers in April and May. It is native to Japan and is grown widely for ornament in Europe. Cultivars with purplish leaves are popular.

Japanese Maple *Acer japonicum* Up to 15m

A small tree with a domed crown and short bole. Bark is grey-brown and the twigs are reddish tinged above. Opposite leaves are 7 to 12cm long and divided into seven to eleven, broadly oval lobes, cut less than halfway to the base; the margins bear sharp, forward-pointing teeth. Reddish flowers are borne in clusters of 9 to 15; each flower is 12 to 15mm across and carried on a long stalk. Paired fruits are 3cm long with widely spreading wings. Flowers in April and May. Native to Japan and is grown in Europe for ornament, some cultivars having good autumn colour.

Red Maple *Acer rubrum* Up to 20m

Best known for its autumn colours this rounded tree has reddish twigs and buds. Opposite leaves are 10cm long and divided into three, sometimes five, broadly oval lobes, cut less than halfway to the base; the margins bear forward-pointing teeth and the petiole is red. Leaves are dark green but turn bright red in autumn. Red flowers, which appear before the leaves, are borne in clusters, the individual flowers being carried on stalks. Paired fruits are 10mm long and red with the wings forming a shallow angle. Flowers in March. Native to North America. Grown in Europe for ornament.

Horse-chestnut *Aesculus hippocastanum* Up to 35m

The familiar conker is a seed from this wide-spreading tree. Bark is brown-grey and the reddish-brown twigs bear large, sticky buds in winter. Opposite leaves are divided into five to seven leaflets, each 10 to 25cm long; they are oval, toothed and bright green. Flowers are borne in erect, conical to pyramidal spikes up to 30cm long. Individual flowers are white, 2cm across with four to five recurved petals and long, downcurved stamens. Fruit, up to 6cm across has a thick, spiny husk containing one or more seeds. Flowers in April and May. Native to the Balkans but widely planted elsewhere.

Red Horse-chestnut *Aesculus × carnea* Up to 30m

Very similar to its parent horse-chestnut, differing mainly in its pink or red flowers. The leaves are divided into five leaflets, each 10 to 25cm long, dark green and oval; typically they droop as though from lack of water. The flowers are borne in erect, conical to pyramidal spikes up to 20cm; individual flowers are pink or red. Fruit is up to 6cm across with a thick but more-or-less smooth husk with few, if any, spines. Flowers in April and May. It is a hybrid between Horse-chestnut and the North American Red Buckeye (*A. pavia*) and is grown for ornament.

Indian Horse-chestnut *Aesculus indica* Up to 20m

A small, delicate tree with a narrow crown. Stout trunk has smooth grey-green or pinkish bark. The opposite leaves are divided into five narrowly-oval leaflets, each 10 to 25cm long and carried on petioles. The flower spikes are 10 to 15cm long, erect and pyramidal. Individual flowers are about 2cm across and white, tinged with pink or yellow. Fruit has a rough, but not spiny, thin husk containing two to three wrinkled, glossy brown seeds. Flowers in June. It is native to the Himalayas and grown in Europe for ornament.

California Buckeye *Aesculus californica* Up to 10m

This small tree has a rounded outline and short bole. Opposite leaves are divided into five or sometimes seven dark green leaflets; these are roughly 10cm long, oval in outline and borne on petioles. The flowers are borne in erect, rounded to conical spikes 15 to 20cm long; individual flowers are about 2cm across, white or pale pink and fragrant with protruding stamens. Fruit is 5 to 7cm long, asymmetrical and with a rough but not spiky husk, splitting to reveal shiny brown nuts. Flowers in June and July. Native to California and is sometimes grown in Europe for ornament.

Bottlebrush Buckeye *Aesculus parviflora* Up to 5m

An attractive, spreading deciduous shrub or small tree. Opposite leaves are divided into five or seven leaflets; these are roughly 10cm long, oval in outline and borne on petioles. In the spring, the leaves are bronzy but turn dark green in the summer; in autumn they turn golden-yellow. Flowers are borne in erect, rounded-conical spikes 10 to 15cm long; individual flowers are red-centred and white. The fruit is 5 to 6cm long and contains shiny brown nuts. Flowers in July and August. Native to North America and is sometimes grown in Europe for ornament.

Tree-of-Heaven *Ailanthus altissima* 20 to 30m

A fast-growing, pollution- and salt-tolerant tree. The straight trunk suckers at the base; bark is grey. Rank-smelling, alternate leaves are 45 to 60cm long, pinnate with 13 to 25 pairs of leaflets. Leaflets are 7 to 12cm long, narrowly oval with two to four small teeth near the base; they unfold red but become green. Flowers are 7 to 8mm across, five-petalled, greenish-white and strongly scented; they occur in large, branched clusters, the sexes borne on separate trees. Fruits are 3 to 4cm long. Native to China and grown in Europe for ornament, especially in parks, and as a street tree or soil stabiliser.

Box *Buxus sempervirens* Up to 5m

A familiar, dense evergreen tree or shrub. Young twigs are green and four-angled, with white hairs. Opposite leaves are 1.5 to 3cm long, oval to oblong, notched with entire, rolled-down margins; they are thick and leathery, dark and glossy above but pale green beneath with white hairs on the basal half. Tight, petal-less axillary flower clusters, 5mm across, contain five to six male flowers surrounding a single female flower. A blue-green capsule, 7mm long, ripens brown before explosively releasing seeds. Flowers in April. It is scattered throughout Europe on chalky soils and grown for hedging and topiary.

Balearic Box *Buxus balearica* Up to 8m

A small, rather upright tree. The bark is pinkish and the twigs are stout and stiff, flattened at the nodes and glabrous. The opposite leaves are 2.5 to 4cm long, oval to oblong with entire, slightly rolled-down margins; they are thick, leathery and dull green. Tight axillary flower clusters, 10mm in diameter contain male flowers surrounding a single female flower. The woody capsule is tipped with long, curved horns. Flowers from May to July. It is native to the Balearic Islands, parts of southern and eastern Spain and Sardinia.

Holly *Ilex aquifolium* 3 to 15m

Associated with Christmas, this small, conical evergreen tree is often only a shrub. Bark is silver-grey and fissured with age; the young branches curve upwards at the tip. Alternate leaves are 5 to 12cm long, stiffly leathery, waxy and wavy with spiny margins; they are dark green and glossy above but paler beneath. Flowers white, 6mm in diameter, four-petalled and borne in axillary clusters; males and females on different trees. Bright red berries are 7 to 12mm long. Flowers from May to August. Native in western and southern Europe and often cultivated. Variegated leaf cultivars are common.

117

Highclere Holly *Ilex × altaclarensis* Up to 20m

A domed, dense-crowned tree with spreading branches. Bark is purplish-grey; twigs have purplish marks. Alternate leaves are up to 9cm long, oval to oblong, flat and entire or with up to ten small, weak, forward-pointing spines on each side. Flowers are up to 12mm long, the five petals white, sometimes tinged purple at the base; male and female flowers occur on different trees. The berry is 12mm long and bright scarlet. Flowers in May. It is a hybrid between Holly and Canary holly (*Ilex perado*) and is often planted in towns being pollution- resistant.

Spindle-tree *Euonymus europaeus* Up to 6m

Normally a slender, twiggy tree or shrub. The twigs are four-angled. Opposite leaves are 3 to 10cm long, elliptical to oval, slightly tapering towards the tip and toothed; they are deep green in summer turning purplish-red in autumn. The inconspicuous flowers have four tiny sepals, four narrow, greenish petals and a green central disc. The pink fruit, 1 to 1.5cm in diameter, is a four-lobed capsule, each lobe containing a single orange seed. Flowers in May and June. Native to most of Europe, occurring mainly on lime-rich soils, and is often planted for ornament.

Christ's Thorn *Paliurus spina-christi* Up to 3m

This spiny tree or shrub has numerous, clinging branches. The flexible twigs have pairs of needle-sharp spiny stipules, one hooked and one straight. Alternate leaves form two rows along the twig; they are 2 to 4cm long, oval and may be either entire or minutely toothed. The yellow, five-petalled flowers are 5mm across and borne in loose axillary clusters. Woody fruits resemble broad-rimmed hats 2 to 3cm across, the brim formed by a wavy, spreading wing. Flowers in July. It is native to hot parts of the Mediterranean and is sometimes used for farm hedges.

Buckthorn *Rhamnus catharticus* 4 to 10m

A spiny tree with opposite branches spreading at right angles. Scaly black bark reveals orange patches. Opposite leaves are in crowded pairs at 90 degrees to each other; they are 3 to 7cm long, oval to elliptical, pointed and finely toothed. The upper surface is dull green, the lower surface is paler with two to four pairs of lateral veins. Fragrant greenish-white flowers are 4mm long, four- or five- petalled, solitary or in clusters, the males and females on different trees. Berry-like fruits are 6 to 8mm across and ripen black. Flowers in May. Native to most of Europe.

Alder-buckthorn *Frangula alnus* Up to 5m

A small tree with opposite branches ascending at a sharp angle. Bark is smooth and the twigs are minutely hairy. Mostly opposite, entire leaves are 2 to 7cm long, widest above the middle with seven to nine pairs of lateral veins curving towards the wavy margins; young leaves are covered with brownish hairs which soon fall. Greenish-white flowers are 3mm across with five, small petals and stout stalks; they form axillary clusters. Berry-like fruit is 10mm across and ripens from green through yellow and red to purplish-black. Flowers mainly in May and June. Native to much of Europe.

Sea-buckthorn *Hippophae rhamnoides* Up to 11m

A densely-branched tree or sprawling shrub. Twigs are thorny and both leaves and twigs are covered with minute either silvery or sometimes brownish scales. Numerous suckers grow from the base of the trunk. The alternate, narrow, drooping leaves are 1 to 6cm long and silvery on both sides, or sometimes dull grey-green above. Greenish flowers are 3mm across and are tubular with two sepals but no petals. They appear in clusters, males and females on different trees. The oval, orange berries are 6 to 8mm across. Flowers in March and April. It is native to much of Europe, mainly on the coast.

Hibiscus *Hibiscus rosa-sinensis* 1 to 3m

A small, spreading evergreen tree or large shrub. Alternate leaves are up to 15cm long, oval, toothed and glossy green. Flowers are usually solitary in axils or the upper leaves. They typically have five spreading petals, 5 to 12cm long and deep red with a darker patch towards the base. Numerous stamens form a distinctive, brush-like column; the style is long with five short branches bearing knob-like stigmas. Fruit is a narrowly ovoid capsule seated in the persistant calyx. Flowers more-or-less all year. Unknown in the wild but cultivated throughout warmer parts of the world.

Small-leaved Lime *Tilia cordata* Up to 30m

A broadly columnar tree with a dense crown of downwardly arching branches. Alternate leaves are 3 to 9cm long, very broadly heart-shaped and finely-toothed; they are dark shiny green above and paler beneath, with tufts of pale red-brown hairs in the vein-axils. The five-petalled flowers are white and fragrant and borne in pendulous clusters of 4 to 15 attached to a pale green, wing-like bract. The thin-shelled, globose nuts are 6mm long, downy at first, becoming glabrous and usually ribbed. Flowers in July. Native to limestone areas in Europe.

Common Lime *Tilia × vulgaris* Up to 45m

A tall tree with a narrow crown. Broad, alternate leaves are 6 to 10cm long with the base heart-shaped or cut straight across; they are dull green above, paler with tufts of white hairs in the vein-axils beneath, and often exude sticky sap. The five-petalled flowers are yellow-white and fragrant with five to ten in pendulous clusters attached to a yellowish-green, wing-like bract. The thick-shelled, ovoid to globose nuts are 8mm long, downy and weakly ribbed. Flowers in July. It is a naturally occurring hybrid between small- and large-leaved limes.

Weeping Silver Lime *Tilia petiolaris* Up to 30m

A tall tree with a domed crown. The branches are ascending at first but the twigs characteristically droop. Broad, alternate leaves are 5 to 12cm long with the base heart-shaped and the margins toothed; they are dark green above and paler with downy white hair beneath. The five-petalled flowers are off-white with three to ten in pendulous clusters attached to a pale green, wing-like bract. The ovoid to globose nuts are 12mm long. Flowers in July. It is possibly native to the Caucasus but is common grown for ornament or as a street tree.

Silver Lime *Tilia tomentosa* Up to 30m

A compact tree with a broadly domed crown and handsome foliage. Alternate leaves are 8 to 10cm long, heart-shaped with an asymmetric base and sharp-toothed margins; they are dark green above and densely silvery white with stellate hairs beneath. Flowers are five-petalled, yellowish or white and fragrant with six to ten in a pendulous cluster attached to a yellowish, wing-like bract. Ovoid nuts are 6 to 12mm long, downy and with five prominent ribs. Flowers in July and August. Native from Hungary eastwards into Asia and is often planted in Europe.

Large-leaved Lime *Tilia platyphyllos* Up to 40m

A tall tree with a narrowly domed crown of ascending branches. Heart-shaped, alternate leaves are 6 to 9cm long, sharply toothed and hairy on both sides, but more so beneath. The five-petalled flowers are yellowish and fragrant with two to six in a long-stalked, pendulous cluster attached to a whitish, wing-like bract. The nuts are globose, 8 to 12mm long and hairy with three to five prominent ribs. Large-leaved lime flowers in June. It is native to hilly regions of central and southern Europe and is planted as a street tree elsewhere.

This tall tree has a broadly conical crown. Bark is grey-brown and ridged. The 5 to 12cm long leaves are oval with a tapering base and margin; hairy on the midrib but otherwise glabrous with a 2cm petiole. Dark green leaves turn red or yellow in autumn. Greenish flowers are 1.5cm across, carried in clusters. Male and female flowers occur on separate trees; male clusters are dense, females clusters less so usually with three flowers in a head. The bluish-black, 1 to 2cm long fruits are borne in small clusters. Native to North America and grown for ornament in Europe.

Pocket-handkerchief Tree *Davidia involucrata* Up to 20m

A broadly-domed tree when mature. The 8 to 17cm long leaves are broadly oval and heart-shaped at the base with sharp-toothed margins; they are dark shiny green above but paler and downy beneath. The flowers are small and lack petals; they occur in dense heads comprising one bisexual flower and numerous males with two large, white, leaf-like bracts up to 15cm long. Rounded fruits are 3cm long and greenish. Flowers in May. Native to China but commonly grown in Europe as an ornamental tree in parks and gardens.

Cider Gum *Eucalyptus gunnii* Up to 30m

A fast-growing evergreen. Greyish bark may persist lower down but usually shreds to leave a smooth green-, pink- or white-tinged trunk. Opposite, almost circular juvenile leaves are 3 to 4cm long and clasp the stem. The alternate adult leaves are up to 7cm long and grey-green. Flowers are white and occur in clusters of three, the buds with shortly beaked caps. The 1cm long fruit has a small, depressed blunt disc and three to five narrowly projecting valves. Flowers in May and June. Native to southern Australia and Tasmania and is planted for ornament in cooler parts of Europe.

Snow Gum *Eucalyptus pauciflora* subsp. *niphophila* Up to 15m

A small, often shrub-like tree with attractive flowers. The bark is grey-green and peels into large flakes. The opposite, almost circular juvenile leaves are 6cm long and tough. The alternate adult leaves are lanceolate, up to 15cm long and glossy green. Flowers are whitish and occur in clusters in the leaf axils. The 6mm long fruit is cup-shaped and is carried on a short stalk. Native to southern Australia, occuring mainly in mountainous regions. In Europe, it is grown as an ornamental tree in cooler regions such as Britain and is a familiar sight in parks and gardens.

Maiden's Gum *Eucalyptus globulus* subsp. *maidenii* Up to 40m

The bluish-white bark of this open-crowned tree is shed annually. Opposite, greyish juvenile leaves are 16cm long, ovate and often heart-shaped at the base. Alternate adult leaves are up to 20cm long, lanceolate, leathery and dark shiny green. White flowers are borne in flat-stalked clusters 10 to 15cm long with three to seven or more flowers. Fruits are 1cm long, bell-shaped or conical with a smooth, thick disc partially fused to the projecting valves. Flowers from March to September. Native to south-eastern Australia and is grown for timber in parts of southern Europe.

Ribbon Gum *Eucalyptus viminalis* Up to 50m

A large evergren with a long, straight and unbranched trunk. Thin outer bark shreds and hangs in ribbons revealing white inner bark beneath. Juvenile leaves are opposite, up to 10cm long, the bases clasping the stem. Adult leaves are alternate, up to 18cm long, narrowly oval with a drawn-out tip. The stalkless flowers are 1.5cm across, creamy white and in clusters of three. The flower buds have scarlet, almost conical caps. Fruit is almost spherical and opens by three to four valves. Flowers from December to June. Native to Australia and grown in Europe for shade and timber.

Pomegranate *Punica granatum* Up to 8m

Cultivated for its fruit, this slender tree has pale brown, grooved, bark. Branches are angled upwards. Opposite leaves are 2 to 8cm long, oblong to narrowly oval but widest above the middle. Flowers are solitary or in pairs at the shoot-tips; the five to seven petals are crumpled before opening and the five to seven hooded, leathery red sepals are joined into a long tuber, persisting on the fruit. Berry-like fruit is 5 to 8cm long, with leather skin and numerous seeds embedded in the pulp. Flowers from June to October. It is an ancient introduction to Europe from Asia.

Cornelian Cherry *Cornus mas* Up to 8m

A small tree or shrub with an open crown, spreading branches and downswept twigs. Opposite leaves are 4 to 10cm long, ovate to elliptical and pointed, yellowish-green and conspicuously veined. The flowers are about 4mm across, four-petalled, bright yellow and appearing before the leaves in axillary clusters 2cm across. The fleshy berry is 12 to 20mm long, oblong and ovoid, bright red and acid-tasting when ripe. Flowers in February and March. It is native to central and south-eastern Europe and is cultivated for ornament and its fruit.

127

Japanese Strawberry Tree *Cornus kousa* Up to 15m

A smallish, columnar deciduous tree. The bark is reddish-brown and peels in older trees. Ovate leaves are 6 to 7.5cm long with a wavy margin and tapering point; the upper surface is dark green and the underside has patches of brown hairs in the vein-axils. The small, yellowish flowers are borne in clusters forming rounded heads. These form stalked clusters of tiny fruits that resemble strawberries. Flowers in June. It is native to mountain slopes in Japan and is grown in Europe as an ornamental tree in gardens and parks.

Snowbell-tree *Styrax japonica* Up to 10m

A small tree with an open crown and spreading branches. The opposite leaves are 10cm long, ovate to elliptical and pointed, glossy green turning red or yellow in autumn, with a finely toothed margin. The flowers are about 15mm across, creamy-white and are pendulous on stalks and in loose clusters; they appear with the leaves. Fruit is ovoid to globose, berry-like and 15mm across, containing a single seed. Flowers in June and July. It is native to China and Japan and is grown as an ornamental tree in northern Europe.

Strawberry-tree *Arbutus unedo* Up to 12m

The distinctive fruit gives this dense, rounded evergreen its name. Fissured red bark flakes into strips from the short trunk. Young twigs are reddish with glandular hairs. Alternate glossy leaves are 4 to 11cm long, oblong-lanceolate, with sharp teeth, those towards the leaf-tip ringed red; the red petiole is 6mm long. The greenish or pinkish-white, 9mm long flowers have a calyx with rounded lobes and an urn-shaped corolla; they are carried in drooping clusters. Fruit is 2cm across, globose, deep red when ripe. Flowers in October and November. Native to the Mediterranean and milder parts of western Europe as far north as Ireland.

Cyprus Strawberry-tree *Arbutus andrachne* Up to 12m

A dense, rounded evergreen with smooth, rich orange-red bark which shreds into papery sheets. The young twigs are glabrous. Alternate leaves are 3 to 6cm long, glossy green and usually entire; the petiole is 15 to 30mm long and green. The flowers are greenish or pinkish, 9mm long, the calyx with round lobes and the corolla urn-shaped; they are carried in erect clusters. Globose fruit is 0.8 to 1.2cm across, orange when ripe with a network or raised lines. Flowers in March and April. It is native to the Aegean region.

129

Rhododendron *Rhododendron ponticum* Up to 5m

This familiar evergreen, shrubby tree has spreading branches. Alternate, leathery leaves are 8 to 25cm long, elliptical to oblong, dark and shiny green above but paler beneath. Flowers are borne in clusters of 8 to 15 on stalks 2 to 6mm long. The calyx is very small and green while the corolla is 4 to 6cm across, broadly bell-shaped, five-lobed and dull or violet-purple. Fruit is a dry capsule containing numerous small, flat seeds. Flowers in May and June. Native to the Himalayas and is grown in Europe for ornament. It is naturalised in many areas.

Manna Ash *Fraxinus ornus* Up to 25m

A domed tree with rather showy blossom. Bark is smooth and grey; the winter buds are grey or brown with a white bloom. Opposite, pinnate leaves, up to 30cm long, have five to nine leaflets each 3 to 10cm long; these are ovate, irregularly toothed and downy with white or brownish hairs on the veins beneath. Flowers are borne in large clusters 15 to 20cm long; they are fragrant and have four narrow petals 5 to 6mm long. Fruits are 1.5 to 2.5cm long, in dense clusters. Flowers in May. Native to central and southern Europe and is planted as a street tree.

Common Ash *Fraxinus excelsior* Up to 40m

Familiar tree with an open, domed crown. Smooth grey bark eventually develops interwoven ridges and the twigs are markedly flattened at the nodes. Winter buds are black and conical. Opposite, pinnate leaves are 20 to 35cm long with 7 to 13 leaflets each 5 to 12cm long, oblong to oval, pointed and toothed; there are dense, white hairs beneath. Flowers appear before leaves in axillary clusters, males and females often on separate twigs. Both sexes are purple and lack sepals and petals. Fruits 2.5 to 5cm long, form dense clusters. Flowers in April and May. Native throughout Europe.

Caucasian Ash *Fraxinus oxycarpa* Up to 25m

This tree has a tall but unkempt crown. Bark is smooth and greyish, becoming ridged with age. Hairy buds are brown. Opposite, pinnate leaves are 20 to 30cm long with 7 to 13 leaflets, each oblong to oval, pointed and toothed. The upper surface is glossy, patches of white hairs are on the base of the midribs beneath. Flowers appear before the leaves in clusters. The winged fruits form dense, hanging clusters. Flowers in May and is native to the Caucasus, Asia Minor and south-eastern Europe. It is sometimes grown elsewhere in Europe as an ornamental tree and cultivars exist.

Olive *Olea europaea* Up to 15m

Cultivated since ancient times, this long-lived evergreen has a broad crown, a gnarled and silvery trunk and the main branches with large cavities and holes. Opposite, leathery leaves are 2 to 8cm long, lanceolate and grey-green above with silver hairs beneath; the petiole is very short. White, fragrant flowers are four-petalled and in loose, many-flowered axillary spikes. Oily-fleshed ovoid fruit is 1 to 3cm long, green in the first year, ripening black in the second; it contains a single large stone. Flowers in July and August. It is native to southern Europe.

Common Privet *Ligustrum vulgare* Up to 10m

A dense, usually deciduous shrub or small tree with spreading branches. The opposite leaves are 3 to 5cm long, oval, entire, thick and leathery; they are very glossy above but paler and matt beneath. The loose, conical flower heads are 7 to 12 cm long and axillary. Flowers are white, heavily scented, the tubular corolla with four spreading lobes. Berries are about 5mm long, oval to globose and black with a white bloom. Flowers from July to September. It is a lime-loving species, native to most of Europe, and is sometimes grown as a hedging plant.

Indian Bean-tree *Catalpa bignoides* Up to 20m

An attractive, broadly domed tree, sometimes grown for ornament. Usually opposite leaves are 10 to 25cm long, oval with a round- or heart-shaped base and short, tapering tip; they may be shallowly lobed and pale green but sometimes purple-tinged when young. Flowers are 5cm across with five frilled white petals spotted with yellow and purple; they are borne in loose, conical clusters 15 to 25cm long. Fruit capsules are 15 to 40cm long and contain papery seeds; they persist on otherwise bare twigs in winter. Flowers from June to August. It is native to North America and planted in Europe.

Yellow Catalpa *Catalpa ovata* Up to 10m

Stunning in flower, this broadly domed tree has usually opposite leaves 25cm long and 25cm across with three or five short-pointed lobes. The leaf base is heart-shaped and the leaf surfaces are dark green. Showy flower heads are up to 25cm long and comprise numerous individual flowers, each 25mm across, yellowish-white and spotted with red. The pendulous fruit capsules are up to 30cm long, very slender and carried in persistant bunches. Flowers in July and August. It is native to China and is grown in Europe as an ornamental tree.

Elder *Sambucus nigra* Up to 10m

This bushy tree or shrub has main branches which curve outwards. Greyish bark is grooved and corky and the twigs have a white central pith. Opposite leaves are pinnate with five to seven leaflets each 4 to 12cm long; these are ovate, sharply toothed, dull green above with sparse hairs beneath, and unpleasant-smelling. Branched, flat-topped flower heads 10 to 24cm across contain numerous small, white, five-petalled flowers; these are headily fragrant but foetid. The whole head nods when black, 6 to 8mm berries are fully ripe. Flowers in June and July. Native to most of Europe.

Guelder-rose *Viburnum opulus* Up to 4m

A small spreading tree with twigs that are angled, greyish and hairy. Opposite leaves are 3 to 8cm long, downy beneath with three or five spreading, irregularly toothed lobes. The five-petalled, white flowers are grouped in 4.5 to 10cm heads comprising sterile 15 to 20mm flowers around the rim and fertile 4 to 7mm flowers in the centre. Globose fruits are 8mm long, translucent red and often persisting on the tree well after the leaves have fallen. Flowers in June and July. It is native to most of Europe, growing in moist wood margins and hedgerows.

134

Wayfaring-tree *Viburnum lantana* Up to 6m

A small, spreading tree or shrub. Cylindrical twigs are greyish with stellate hairs. Opposite leaves are 4 to 14cm long, oval, shortly and finely toothed, rough and grey-green; there are sparse stellate hairs, especially beneath. Flower heads are 6 to 10cm across, branched, domed and many-flowered. Individual flowers are 5 to 9mm across, five-petalled and white. Fruits are 8mm long, oval, red at first but ripening suddenly but not simultaneously black. Flowers in May and June. It is native to Europe as far north as Britain and Scandinavia, preferring chalky soils.

Cabbage Palm *Cordyline australis* Up to 13m

A palm-like evergreen with bare, forked trunks often suckering and forming clumps. Bark is brown or greyish and cracked into a regular pattern of squares. Leaves are 30 to 90cm long, hard and sharp-pointed, dark green or tinged yellow; they top the trunks in dense tufts, the youngest leaves erect, the oldest hanging down and obscuring the trunk. The fragrant flowers are about 1cm across, creamy white and carried in a huge, branched cluster 60 to 120cm long, growing from the centre of the crown. Berries are 6mm across, globose and usually bluish-white. Native to New Zealand and grown for ornament in Europe.

Spanish Bayonet *Yucca aloifolia* Up to 10m

A robust, palm-like evergreen with a smooth, stout trunk and much-branched crown. The stiff bluish-green leaves form tufts at the tips of the branches. They are 50 to 100cm long, sword-shaped with shortly-toothed margins. The white flowers are 4 to 6cm long and the perianth is bell-shaped with six purple-tinged lobes. Edible fruit is elongated, ripening purplish black. Flowers in April and May. It is native to southern North America and the West Indies and is grown for ornament in southern Europe and coastal western Europe.

Banana *Musa acuminata* Up to 3m

Strictly a giant herb, growing from a horizontal, underground stem. Hollow, aerial 'stem' comprises closely sheathed leaf bases. The crown is formed of oar-shaped leaf blades 120 to 200 cm long. Complex inflorescence is 100cm long and grows up through the 'stem', emerging and drooping. Sheathing, purplish bracts peel to reveal the flowers. Male flowers are borne towards the tip with females in rings below. Fruit is the well-known banana. Flowers from March to September. Native to Asia but cultivars are grown in coastal parts of the Mediterranean.

European Fan Palm *Chamaerops humilis* Up to 2m

A dwarf palm with stiff, fan-shaped leaves. The thick trunks covered in fibre usually form clumps but may be absent in wild plants. The stiff, bluish-green leaves are 100cm across and deeply divided into narrow, tapering segments, forked or notched at the tip. Old leaf bases persist as whitish fibres on the trunk. The bright yellow male and greenish female flowers are usually on different trees; they occur in branched clusters 35cm long. The globose fruits are up to 45mm across and yellowish or brown. Flowers from March to June. It is Europe's only native palm, occuring mainly in western Mediterranean regions.

California Fan Palm *Washingtonia filifera* Up to 15m

A fast-growing palm with a thick trunk slightly swollen at the base. Grey, ringed bark is usually hidden by a skirt of dead leaves. The grey-green leaves are 150 to 200cm long and divided at least halfway into narrow, two-lobed and drooping segments joined by fine, white threads. The slender, branched flower clusters are 300 to 500cm long and arch down from the crown. Flowers are numerous and white. Fruit is 6mm long, ovoid and brownish-black when ripe. Flowers from March to June. It is native to southern North America and planted in Mediterranean regions.

Chinese Windmill Palm *Trachycarpus fortunei* Up to 14m

A compact palm with a brown, shaggy trunk covered with the matted, fibrous bases of dead leaves on the upper part. The fan-shaped or circular leaves are up to 100cm across and divided almost to the base into stiff, narrow, pleated segments. The many-branched, conical flower clusters are 70 to 80cm long and are sheathed with bracts; the flowers are yellow and fragrant. The three-lobed fruits are 2cm long and purplish to white. Flowers from March to June. Native to China and grown for ornament mainly around the Mediterranean.

Date Palm *Phoenix dactylifera* Up to 35m

A slender palm producing delicious fruit. It suckers freely at the base but these are usually cut away in cultivated trees. The crown is thin, with only 20 to 40 grey to green leaves each up to 400cm long. Leaflets are 30 to 40cm long and radiate in all planes, those nearest the base of the leaf viciously spiny. The broom-like flower clusters are numerous, each up to 200cm long with a single, sheathing bract. Fruits are 2.5 to 7cm long, usually orange when ripe, fleshy and sweet. Flowers in April and May. Planted in southern Europe for its popular and delicious fruit.

Canary Island Date Palm *Phoenix canariensis* Up to 20m

A stout palm, its trunk becoming scarred from old leaf bases and there is a dense crown of over 100 leaves. The pinnate leaves reach 5 to 6m in length with numerous V-shaped leaflets 40 to 50cm long, radiating in all planes and spiny near the leaf base. Flower clusters are numerous, each up to 200cm long with a single, sheathing bract; male and female flowers occur on different trees. The inedible, orange or purplish fruits are about 2cm long and hang in massive clusters from the crown. Flowers from March to May. Native to the Canary Islands and planted around the Mediterranean.

Chilean Wine Palm *Jubaea chilensis* Up to 30m

A large, slow-growing palm. The trunk is up to 200cm in diameter and the lead-grey bark is marked with diamond-shaped leaf-scars. The leaves are up to 400cm long, erect and arranged in nearly vertical rows; the leaflets are numerous and arranged in two rows. Erect flower clusters are about 150cm long with a persistant, sheathing bract. Flowers are purplish, males and females in the same clusters. Fruits are 4 to 5cm across, globose, pale yellow and fleshy when ripe. Flowers from July to September. Native to a small, coastal area of Chile and grown for ornament around the Mediterranean.

Further reading

The following list of books are just a few of the many dealing with various aspects of trees.

Cleave, A.J. *Field Guide to the Trees of Britain, Europe and North America*. The Crowood Press, Ramsbury, 1994

Edlin, H.L. *The Natural History of Trees*. Weidenfeld and Nicolson, London. 1976

Krussman, G. *Manual of Cultivated Broad-leaved Trees and Shrubs*. Batsford, London, 1984–1986

Meikle, R.D. *Willows and Poplars of Great Britain and Ireland*. Botanical Society of the British Isles, London, 1984

Press, J.R. and Hosking, D. *Photographic Field Guide to the Trees of Britain and Europe*. New Holland, London, 1993.

Useful addresses

Arboricultural Association
Brokerswood House, Brokerswood, Nr Westbury, Wilts
BA13 4EH

Council for the Protection of Rural England
4 Hobart Place, London SW1W 0HY

Countryside Commission
John Dower House, Crescent Place, Cheltenham, Glos
GL50 3RA

International Union for the Conservation of Natural
Resources (IUCN)
Avenue du Mont Blanc, CH-1196, Gland, Switzerland

National Trust
42 Queen Anne's Gate, London SW1H 9AS

Royal Forestry Society
102 High Street, Tring, Herts HP23 4AH

Tree Council
35 Belgrave Square, London SW1X 8QN

The Wildlife Trusts (RSNC)
The Green, Witham Park, Waterside South,
Lincoln LN2 5JR

Index

141

42355